RECIPES

from

SCOTLAND

F. MARIAN McNEILL

THE ALBYN PRESS
CHARLES SKILTON PUBLISHING GROUP
3 ABBEYMOUNT, EDINBURGH

FIRST PUBLISHED 1946
SECOND EDITION 1947
THIRD EDITION 1952
FOURTH EDITION 1956
FIFTH EDITION 1960
SIXTH EDITION 1963
SEVENTH EDITION 1965
EIGHTH EDITION 1967
NINTH EDITION 1969
TENTH EDITION 1971
ELEVENTH EDITION 1972
TWELFTH EDITION 1973

THE ALBYN PRESS
RAEBURN HOUSE
3 ABBEYMOUNT
EDINBURGH
SCOTLAND
AND AT
90 THE BROADWAY
LONDON SW19

Printed in Scotland by
THE STANLEY PRESS, EDINBURGH

CONTENTS

INTRODUCTION

In an earlier book, *The Scots Kitchen*, I published a number of recipes collected from old Scottish cookery-books and oral tradition, together with an historical introduction, copious notes, and literary allusions to individual dishes. The aim of this little book is more limited and more precise : it is simply a practical cookery-book designed primarily for visitors to Scotland, " lost " Scots, and others who might like to try out some of our Scottish dishes in their own homes ; though at the same time I hope it may do something towards fostering a healthy nationalism in the Scottish kitchen. A certain number of dishes reappear in these pages, but for the authentic old recipes I have substituted simplified and modernised versions—except for bannocks, brose, and similar plain but-and-ben recipes, which cannot be simplified—whilst the majority of the recipes are new. They are all, to the best of my belief, either dishes of Scottish origin, or dishes common to the British Isles but having a definite Scottish accent.

Although our basic Scottish fare differs from that of England quite as markedly as the basic fare of, say France differs from that of Spain, it is not always easy for the uninitiated to discriminate between Scottish and English dishes. For this there are two main reasons. First, there is the widely prevalent habit among writers on English (as distinct from British or general) cookery to include any Scottish dishes that take their fancy, with or without acknowledgment to Scotland. Even the late Miss Florence White, who does discriminate between the two cuisines, and whose excellent *Good Things in England* is ostensibly confined to England, cannot resist an occasional raid over the Border in quest of a haggis or other small game !

7

It is more surprising to find that distinguished gastronome, M. André Simon, arguing with a curiously un-French disregard of logic—are the London fogs to blame?—that because the Scots speak the English language therefore it is right and proper to include Scottish dishes under the title " English Fare." One might as well argue that the term " Church of England " covers the Church of Scotland, or that " English Constitutional Law " covers Scottish constitutional law, though they are as different as chalk from cheese ; and he would be a rash man who described a Scottish Rugger " International " team as a group of English footballers ! Why, even to describe Scottish porridge as English porridge is an injustice to Scotland ! Many good things come out of England, but porridge, as it happens, is not one of them. But apparently the smaller nations are liable to such annoying, if flattering, attentions at the hands of their big neighbours. Even Hungary—so I am told by a Hungarian friend—which possesses one of the finest cuisines in Europe, has the mortification of seeing some of her best dishes presented to the world as Viennese. And, of course, the *haute cuisine* of France is not, like her admirable bourgeois cookery, basically French, but cosmopolitan.

Well, that's one reason. The other is that in the last two generations many Scottish dishes, particularly cakes, scones, and teabread—for as a nation we are definitely better bakers than cooks—have been popularised in England by Scottish writers of general cookery-books, such as Miss Florence Jack (a former principal of the Edinburgh School of the Domestic Arts), author of *Cookery for Every Household* and of the original *Good Housekeeping Cookery Book* ; Mrs Kirk of *Tried Favourites* fame ; Miss Elizabeth Craig, who has written a whole series of best-sellers ; and Mrs Elizabeth Hughes Hallett of *The Hostess Book*, to mention only a few.

Like every other art, the cookery of a nation always has its roots in the soil ; it draws its basic materials from the soil, and its basic methods from those who have lived longest on the soil, and who thus know best how to use its products. The basis of Scottish cookery is, broadly speaking, meal and fish ; the basis of English cookery, flour and meat. The basic kitchen utensils in Scotland are the kail-pot (kail is a synonym for broth), the brander, and the girdle ; in England they are the frying

8

pan and the oven. The kail-pot that has simmered for centuries hung on a chain over the glowing peat-fire in the crofter's kitchen has produced many delectable broths and soups and many a savoury stew. Fish, cured in the traditional way with a touch of the elements—wind-blown, rizzared (sun-dried), rock-dried, or (as with skate), left for a day or two between two grassy sods ; or with a touch of the forest—smoked over oak or silver-birch—or of the sea—smoked over dried sea-weed : all these were cooked on the brander and served simply with butter and bannocks or potatoes. Then the girdle produced the barley bannocks and crisp, nuttily flavoured oatcakes that have been from time immemorial the daily bread of a virile and highly intelligent race.

The diet of the English peasantry, particularly in the south, was less satisfactory, soups being unknown, and the poorest labourers subsisting (says Eden) on " the unvarying meal of dry bread and cheese." On the farm, however, it was another story, and how good English farmhouse cookery can be, both Miss Florence White and Mrs Arthur Webb have amply demonstrated. North of the Border our farmers' wives have shown no less resource and initiative ; but if they still excel in soups and stews, they remain, on the whole, less skilled than the English countrywoman in the art of roasting.

Although a large number of identical food-stuffs are produced all over the British Isles, there are, nevertheless, many differences, due to variations in soil and climate. We cannot, for instance, grow either wheat or the larger fruits to the same perfection as they do in England (except in a few favoured districts), nor are our harvests so certain. But in other respects Nature has been bountiful. Our berry fruits and our tomatoes are full of flavour, due to their slow ripening, and our Midlothian oats are unexcelled in quality. We produce the best beef in the world—that of the Aberdeen-Angus cattle ; our mountain mutton is on a par with that of the English South Down and the Pré-salé of France ; we have venison and feathered game in abundance, including the exquisitely flavoured red grouse, which is peculiar to Scotland and the North of England ; our lochs, rivers, and streams teem with salmon and trout, and our seas with fish—the plump Loch Fynes being by general consent the world's best herring. In short, Scotland is a land of milk and honey—heather honey to boot!—and is able not only to produce all the food she requires, but to export a considerable surplus to England and elsewhere.

What are the predominant characteristics of Scottish cookery? Of our basic cookery, at least, I should say: simplicity, good sense, and an instinct for dietetic values. Travellers of many generations have remarked on the fine physique and robust health of the common people. (To-day, alas, this applies only to the country folk, for in the industrial areas slums and cheap imported food have played havoc with both health and physique—an evil with which we are only now beginning to cope seriously.) "Meg Dods" (Mrs Johnston), a contemporary and friend of Sir Walter Scott, and author of a classical work on cookery, while admitting that "the Scots may, and do, fail in a grand dinner, no doubt of it," maintains that nevertheless "as a nation, they manage better than most of their neighbours." Professor Saintsbury, as distinguished a critic of food and drink as of letters, expresses the opinion, after several years' residence in Edinburgh, that "generally speaking, Scotch ideas on food are sound," and that people who turn up their nose at haggis and sheep's head "are, begging their pardon, fools." Lastly, let me quote H. V. Morton, who writes on the completion of his tour in search of Scotland, that it is "the best place in the world to take an appetite." France, he remarks, is all very well for the man who has to be "led gently to his food," but "if a man has an honest appetite sharpened by the open air, he will satisfy it with less risk to his mechanism more speedily in a Scottish kitchen than elsewhere."

These are not extravagant, but they are satisfactory tributes.

The meals we excel in in Scotland are undoubtedly breakfast and tea—the pre-war breakfast, with its porridge and cream, its floury baps, its barley bannocks, its crisp oatcakes, its choice of hot, appetising dishes, its butter, honey and marmalade, its fragrant tea (its coffee, it must be admitted, is a matter of luck); the farmhouse tea, with its variety of scones and teabread, its velvet-textured sponges, its thick crisp shortbread, its rich fruit cake, its jams and jellies of every description. It is not surprising that Scotland—Glasgow to be precise—is the original home of the tea-room.

Our two great gifts to the world's breakfast-table are porridge and orange marmalade. Among other dishes that have achieved a reputation beyond our borders are Barley Broth (better known as Scotch Broth), Cock-a-leekie, and Hotch Potch (the soup that lured Queen Victoria's Prince Consort to the galley of a Highland loch steamer to inquire what was " intill't ") ; Loch Fyne Kippers, Finnan-Haddies (haddocks originally smoked in the village of Findon, near Aberdeen) ; Arbroath Smokies (" closed " haddocks), and Smoked Salmon ; Haggis, Mince, and Small Mutton Pies ; Shortbread—" the triumph of the Scottish bakers' art "—Dundee Cake, and a great variety of Scones. (The word derives from the Gaelic *sgonn*, and should, incidentally, rhyme with *gone*, not with *bone*.) Lastly, we have contributed two standard sauces to Anglo-Celtic (usually misnamed Anglo-Saxon) civilisation—Egg Sauce and Bread Sauce. For most of these dishes, and for many more, the gentle reader is invited to enquire within.

F. Marian McNeill.

SOME SCOTTISH CULINARY TERMS

Ashet	.. ..	A flat, oval serving-dish (Fr. *assiette*).
Baller	.. ..	Balls (Shetland).
Bannock	.. ..	A flat round cake of dough, usually the size of a meat-plate, baked on the girdle.
Bap	.. ..	The traditional breakfast roll of Scotland, oval-shaped, with a dent in the centre.
Bawd	.. ..	A hare.
Blaeberry	.. ..	Bilberry, whortleberry.
Blawn	.. ..	Wind-blown (of fish) ; hung up in a breeze or a current of air.
Bree	.. ..	Pot liquor ; stock ; soup.
Brochan	.. ..	Gruel or porridge.
Brose	.. ..	A dish made by pouring *boiling* water or stock over raw or lightly toasted oatmeal.
Car-cakes	.. ..	Pancakes (A.-S. *keren*, to toss).
Cookie	.. ..	A kind of bun (Flem.).
Crappin	.. ..	Stuffing.
Crappit Heids	..	Stuffed heads (of haddocks, etc.).
Crowdie (1)	.. ..	Highland cream cheese (Gael. *cruth*, curd).
Crowdie (2)	.. ..	A dish made by pouring *cold* water, milk, ale, etc., over raw or lightly toasted oatmeal.
Cuith, cuddie	.. ..	The young of coalfish in their second season. (Gael. *cudaig*.)
Farl	.. ..	A section of an oat bannock quartered before being fired (A.-S. *feorth-dael*, quarter).
Flory	.. ..	A plate-pie, *i.e.*, with pastry above and below the filling.
Gigot	.. ..	A leg of mutton (Fr. *gigot*).
Hough	.. ..	Shin of beef.
Kail	.. ..	The cabbage family. Used also as a synonym for broth, of which cabbage is a main ingredient.
Kipper	.. ..	To cure (salmon, herring, etc.) by salting and smoking.
Lithe	.. ..	To thicken and mellow (of slow-simmering broth).
Parlie	.. ..	Dim. of Parliament Cake, said to have been popular with members of the old Scottish Parliament.
Partan	.. ..	The large edible crab (Gael. *partan*).
Pot-Posy	.. ..	*Bouquet garni* or bunch of herbs for flavouring soups and stews.
Scone	.. ..	Bannock dough cut into small sections or rounds and baked on the girdle or in the oven (Gael. *sgonn*, a section or large mouthful).
Sillock	.. ..	Fry of coalfish (allied to cod).
Stoved	.. ..	A kind of stewing (Fr. *étuvée*).
Sybo	.. ..	Spring onion.
Tattie	.. ..	Potato.
Treacle	.. ..	(Black treacle, to be distinguished from golden syrup) is more commonly known overseas as molasses.

SOUPS

BARLEY BROTH
(SCOTS BROTH)

1½ lbs. Neck of Mutton.	1 breakfastcupful Diced Turnip.
2 oz. Pot Barley.	1 breakfastcupful Diced Carrot.
2 oz. Peas.	1 Grated Carrot.
1 Onion.	1 tablespoonful Chopped Parsley.
White of 1 Leek.	Salt.
½ Small White Heart of Cabbage.	Pepper.
	2 quarts Water.

Wash the peas and soak overnight. (Use fresh ones, of course, in season.) Wipe and trim the meat, and put into the broth-pot with cold water, peas, barley, and salt. Bring to boiling-point and skim. Cut up the leek and onion and add with the diced turnip and carrot. Simmer slowly for three-four hours. Add the shredded cabbage and grated carrot, and simmer half an hour longer. Just before serving, add the parsley. Add pepper and more salt if required, and serve very hot.

Barley broth proper is made with mutton, but excellent broth can be made with a marrow-bone or with runner of beef. Turnip, carrot, and parsley have an affinity with mutton, but with beef the vegetables should be varied a little, e.g., kail, or greens, roughly shredded, may be substituted for the white cabbage, and a stick or two of celery for the parsley ; and more leek may be added. But there are endless variations.

The meat should be removed when ready, and returned to the pot later to heat through. Garnish the mutton with slices of turnip and carrot boiled in the broth, and serve with caper or nasturtium seed sauce. Hodgils (q.v.) or dumplings may be boiled with the beef.

HOTCH-POTCH
OR HARVEST BROTH

2-3 lbs. Neck of Lamb or a Marrow Bone.	1 Lettuce.
1½ pints Fresh Green Peas.	6 Young Turnips.
½ pint Broad Beans.	6 Young Carrots.
1 Cauliflower.	6 Spring Onions.
	6 Sprigs Parsley.

2½ quarts Water.

Put the neck of lamb or the marrow-bone into the broth-pot with the cold water and a little salt. Bring to the boil, and skim carefully. Shell the peas ; shell and skin the beans ; prepare and dice the turnips and carrots ; peel and cut up the onions. Retain half a pint of peas, and put the rest of the prepared vegetables into the boiling liquor. Draw to the side and simmer very gently for three or four hours or longer. It can hardly be cooked too slowly or too long. Meanwhile put the cauliflower and the lettuce into cold water with a little salt, and let them lie for half an hour. Then break the cauli-flower into sprigs and chop the lettuce ; and, half an hour before serving, add them to the broth with the remainder of the peas. Just before serving add the parsley, finely chopped. The soup should be nearly as thick as porridge, and is a meal in itself.

This soup is made only when the kitchen garden is in its prime, and the sweet juices of the young vegetables impart to it a delicious flavour and aroma.

POWSOWDIE
(SHEEP'S HEAD BROTH)

1 Sheep's Head (Singed).	2 tablespoonfuls Fine Oat-meal.
1½ lbs. Mixed Vegetables: Turnip, Carrot, Potato, Leek, Onion.	4 oz. Pot Barley.
	6 Peppercorns.
1 tablespoonful Parsley.	Salt and Pepper.

3 quarts Water.

Choose a fat, round head. The head and feet are not skinned, as in England, but the wool is *singed* off. (This used to be done by the blacksmith, but may be done at home with a red-hot poker ; but it must be done thoroughly.) On this depends the delectable flavour of the broth.

Soak the head overnight in lukewarm water. Take out the glassy part of the eye, scrape the head and brush till perfectly clean and white ; then split it with a cleaver, and lay aside the brains, etc., and clean the nostrils and gristly parts. Wash the head once more, and let it blanch for the pot. Then put it on in cold water along with the barley. Bring to the boil, remove the scum carefully and add salt. After it has boiled for an hour add the vegetables and peppercorns, and simmer very gently for two-three hours longer, according to the size and age of the head. Half an hour before serving, add the oatmeal. Season, and add the parsley last thing ; and, of course, remove the peppercorns.

The head can be served separately with brain sauce, the brains, washed and dried, being tied in muslin and boiled with the head for twenty minutes. Or it can be made into brawn or a ragoût.

COCK-A-LEEKIE

A plump Cock or Fowl.
2 or 3 Bunches of Leeks.
1 dozen Prunes (optional).
Jamaica Pepper.

2 quarts Stock (Beef or Veal) or Water.
Salt.

Truss the fowl, and place in a large pot with the stock and three or four leeks, blanched and chopped. Bring to the boil and cook gently for two hours or until the fowl is tender, when it should be removed. Clear all the grease off with paper. Add the leeks, washed, blanched (if old and strong), and cut into inch-lengths, with more salt if required, and Jamaica pepper to taste. Simmer very gently until the leeks are tender. Half an hour before serving, the prunes (if desired) should be added whole. Nowadays they are usually omitted. A little minced fowl may be added to the soup.

If water is used in place of stock, add a clove, a blade of mace, a sprig of parsley, and six peppercorns tied in muslin, and remove along with the fowl.

Although not in the tradition, some cooks add two table-spoonfuls of rice.

B

FEATHER FOWLIE
(AN OLD SCOTS CHICKEN SOUP)

1 Plump Fowl.	1 dessertspoonful Chopped
A Slice of Ham.	Parsley.
A Pot-Posy:	Salt.
2 Sprigs Parsley.	Pepper.
1 Sprig Thyme.	1 quart Water.
1 Blade Mace.	1 ladleful First Stock.
1 Onion (Medium).	2-3 Egg Yolks.
1 Stick Celery.	1 dessertspoonful Cream.

Joint the fowl, and let the pieces soak for half an hour in water to cover, with a dessertspoonful of salt; then wash well and put into a stewpan with the ham, chopped celery, sliced onion, herbs, and water. Cover, and bring to the boil; then draw to the side and cook gently for 1½ hours. Strain, and remove all grease. Return the soup to the rinsed pan, and add the stock. Heat it up for fifteen minutes, then add the parsley and some of the minced white meat of the fowl. Remove from the fire, stir in the strained egg yolks and the warmed cream, and pour into a heated tureen.

The remainder of the fowl may be served with egg or parsley or bread sauce and curled rashers of bacon, or it may be made into patties.

BAWD BREE
(SCOTS HARE SOUP)

1 Hare.	1 Blade Mace.
1 Hough (Shin) Bone.	12 Peppercorns.
1 Thick Slice Turnip.	2 oz. Bacon Fat or Dripping.
1-2 Carrots.	2 tablespoonfuls Fine Oatmeal.
2 Onions.	2 tablespoonfuls Mushroom Ketchup.
1 Stick Celery.	Salt.
A Pot-Posy:	Cayenne.
1 Sprig Parsley.	3-4 quarts Water.
1 Sprig Thyme.	1-2 glasses Port Wine (optional).
¼ Bay Leaf.	

Prepare the hare the day before it is required. Skin it and clean it thoroughly. Remove the lungs, and be careful not to break the inside. Hold the hare over a basin to catch all the blood, which contains much of the flavour of the hare. Wipe carefully with a damp cloth to remove any small hairs that may adhere. Remove the best part of the flesh from the head, back, shoulders, and rump. Place the remainder in a deep dish, cover with the cold water, and leave overnight. Next day, strain the red water into the broth-pot, add the hare, and bring slowly to the boil. Add the prepared vegetables, cut up roughly, the herbs, mace, and peppercorns (tied together in muslin), and salt to taste. Simmer for two-three hours according to the size and age of the hare. Strain the soup, rubbing the vegetables through the colander with the back of a wooden spoon, and return to the pot.

Meanwhile, while the soup is simmering, flatten some or all the pieces of hare you have set aside, season with salt and pepper, dredge with flour, and fry in the hot bacon fat. (If the hare is large and fleshy some of the pieces may be preserved for hare cakes (q.v.).) Parboil the liver, and pound it in a mortar along with some of the fried hare, then rub through a sieve, or chop small, and add to the soup, together with a handful of lightly toasted oatmeal. Simmer for at least half an hour.

Strain the blood into a small bowl, adding a little cold water ; then rub the flour into it and mix with a teacupful of hot soup, as if making starch. Add more hot soup, and pour gradually into the pot, stirring carefully one way. Keep it just at boiling-point for ten minutes, being careful not to let it curdle. Withdraw, skim, and add any more salt required, the mushroom ketchup, and a pinch of cayenne. A glass or two of port wine enriches the flavour.

Some housewives put a little rowan jelly into the tureen before dishing the soup, and in farmhouses a mealy potato is served in each plateful.

A simple hare soup is made with the thinnest parts of the hare, boiled for 2½ hours in a quart of water with turnip, carrot, and sliced onion, thickened with oatmeal, and seasoned generously ; and (most important) the blood is added as above.

POTATO SOUP

2 lbs. Potatoes.	Salt and Pepper.
½ lb. Onions.	1 teaspoonful Sugar.
¼ lb. Carrots.	3 quarts Bone Stock.

Stock made from the bones of cold roast mutton is excellent for this soup. Tripe stock is also good. If you have no stock, use water, adding 1 lb. neck of mutton. Put the bones or meat on with cold water, and bring slowly to the boil. Remove any scum. Simmer for one hour. Peal and slice the potatoes, chop the onions, and grate the carrots. Add to the soup with salt and sugar, bring to the boil, and simmer steadily for $1\frac{1}{2}$ hours. Add pepper and a scrap of butter or dripping if liked.

In spring and early summer, a handful of young nettle tops, finely chopped, is sometimes added to the soup ten minutes before it is to be dished. Nettles combine well with potato.

LEEK AND POTATO SOUP

I Bunch of Leeks.	Salt.
I lb. Potatoes.	Pepper.
2 oz. Butter or Fat.	I gill Milk-and-Water.
I oz. Flour.	3 pints Bone or Vegetable
A tiny pinch of Mace.	Stock.

Trim the leeks; wash them thoroughly; cut them into three lengthwise, and then across into one-inch lengths. Peel and dice the potatoes. Melt the butter and fry the leeks until lightly coloured. Add the potatoes and cook for a few minutes without colouring. Sprinkle lightly with salt. Pour on the stock, cover the pan, and simmer gently for an hour.

Put an ounce of butter into a small saucepan with the milk-and-water, and when it boils add the flour. Stir over the fire till thick enough to roll up into a ball. Cook for a few minutes on a gentle heat, stirring constantly; then stir in sufficient hot stock to slacken to a pouring consistency. Pour this into the soup, stirring till it comes to the boil. Season well with salt and pepper, and serve piping hot.

RED POTTAGE

I lb. Haricot Beans.	Salt and Pepper.
6 Tomatoes.	2 oz. Butter or
I large Beetroot.	Dripping.
I-2 Onions.	3-4 quarts Water or
I Stick Celery.	Stock.

Wash and soak the beans. Prepare the vegetables; then slice the onions and cut up the others. Heat the fat in a saucepan and sweat the beans and vegetables in it for a few minutes.

Add the liquid and salt to taste, bring to the boil, skim if necessary, and simmer for three-four hours. Remove the beetroot, and rub the remaining contents of the pot through a sieve. Season, re-heat, and serve.

Lentils may be substituted for haricot beans, and parsnip for celery.

KAIL BROSE

A piece of Ox Head or
A Cow Heel or
A piece of Hough.
A Stock of Curly Kail.

1 teacupful Oatmeal.
Salt.
Pepper.
Water.

This dish requires a fatty stock. Boil the ox head (with salt) in water to cover until the fat floats on the top. Take a good stock of curly kail—this is best when it has been touched by frost—wash it carefully, shred it very small, and cook in the stock for ten-fifteen minutes or till tender. Toast the oatmeal lightly in the oven or under the grill, put it into a bowl with a pinch of salt, dash upon it a teacupful of the fat top of the broth, and stir up into knots.

Turn this back into the pot (after removing the meat) and leave for a moment or two before removing from the heat. Stir well, and serve very hot.

ARBROATH FISH SOUP

1 Cod's Head or
2-3 Haddocks' Heads.
2 Onions.
1 small Carrot.
1 Slice Turnip.
1 Stick Celery.
4 oz. Flour.

A Pot-Posy:
  2 Sprigs Parsley, 1 Bay Leaf,
  1 Blade Mace.
Salt and Pepper.
1 oz. Butter.
1 pint Milk.
1 quart Water.

A small Slice of Fish (optional).

Wash the head and put it on with cold water and a little salt. Bring slowly to the boil, and remove the scum. Add the prepared vegetables and the pot posy. Simmer 1½ hours or longer, and strain. Season. Remove skin and bone from the slice of fish, chop small, add to the stock, and cook for five minutes. (Two tablespoonfuls is enough.)

Melt the butter, stir in the flour, and fry for a minute, then add the milk by degrees, and cook, always stirring, for ten minutes. Stir slowly into the soup, and add a tablespoonful of finely minced parsley just before dishing up.

For a richer soup, mix the yolk of an egg with two tablespoonfuls of cream and stir in last thing, but don't let it boil.

A SIMPLE FISH SOUP

3 pints Fish Stock.	I oz. Butter.
½ pint Milk.	2 teaspoonfuls Chopped Parsley.
2 oz. Flour.	Salt and Pepper.

Melt the butter; add the flour and fry a minute, then slowly stir in the stock. Boil for twenty minutes, then add milk, parsley, and seasonings. Boil up and serve.

An excellent soup is made with cuiths or piltocks (as they are variously known)—the young of the saith in their second season. They have an agreeable oysterish flavour, and some aver that piltock soup is as good as oyster soup.

SALMON SOUP

Trimmings of a Fresh Salmon.	I small Carrot.
Bones of I or 2 Fresh Whiting.	I slice Turnip.
I tablespoonful Chopped Parsley.	I stick Celery.
A handful of Brown Breadcrumbs.	I small Onion.
Potato Flour or Mashed Potato.	Water.
Small Slice Fresh Salmon.	

Put into your fish kettle the head, bones, fins, and skins of the salmon, along with the bones of the whiting (these make all the difference) and the prepared vegetables. Cover amply with cold water, bring to the boil, add salt, and boil gently for at least an hour. Strain, and remove all fat and oil. Thicken with potato flour or mashed potato. Add some scallops of uncooked salmon, the chopped parsley, and the brown breadcrumbs. As soon as the salmon is cooked, the soup is ready.

CULLEN SKINK
(FROM THE SHORES OF THE MORAY FIRTH)

A Smoked Haddock.	**I pint Milk.**
I Onion.	**Water.**
I oz. Butter.	**Mashed Potato.**
Salt and Pepper.	

Skin a smoked (preferably Findon) haddock, and place in a pan with just enough boiling water to cover it. Bring to the boil and add a chopped onion. When the haddock is cooked, take it out and remove all the bones. Flake the fish and return the bones to the stock. Boil for one hour. Strain the stock, and bring again to the boil. Bring the milk to the boil in another pan, and add it to the stock with the flaked fish. Add salt to taste, and boil for a few minutes. Add enough mashed potato to make the soup of a nice consistency, with the butter and pepper to taste, and serve.

PARTAN BREE

I good-sized Crab.	**I pint White Stock.**
2¼ oz. Rice.	**Salt.**
I pint Milk.	**White Pepper.**
I gill Cream.	**Anchovy Paste.**

Pick all the meat from a boiled partan (a partan is the large edible crab) and set aside that from the large claws. Boil rice in milk till tender, then pass it along with the crab-meat through a tammy into a basin, and stir with a wooden spoon till perfectly smooth. Add the stock gradually, then the seasonings; put all into a pan and stir over the fire until it approaches boiling-point, but do not let it boil. Add the chopped meat from the claws, and just before serving stir in the cream.

FISH

TO FRY HERRING
(FISHERWIFE'S FASHION)

Herring.
Coarse Oatmeal.

Salt and Pepper.
Dripping.

Remove the heads, fins, and tails with a pair of scissors. Gut, if necessary, remove the scales, and wipe, but do not wash the fish. Score across on both sides, or split and bone them. They should be very dry, and to ensure this, may be left for an hour or more in the folds of a towel. Then sprinkle with salt and pepper, and dip in coarse oatmeal, pressing it on until the fish are completely coated.

Melt a little dripping in a frying-pan, and, when it is smoking hot, put in the fish and fry on both sides (skin side first, if split) until nicely browned and cooked through—about six to ten minutes. Drain, and serve very hot.

TATTIES AN' HERRIN'

Herring.
Potatoes.

Salt.
Water.

Fill a pot nearly full with potatoes, either peeled or (in the old tradition) merely scrubbed. Bring to the boil, and, when the potatoes are half-cooked, pour off most of the water. Return the pot to the fire, place the herring carefully over the potatoes, cover closely, and cook in the steam till ready. Lift on to a hot ashet, and steam the potatoes till dry and mealy.

POTTED HERRINGS

6 Herrings.	18 Peppercorns.
2 Bay Leaves.	Salt and Pepper.
4 Cloves.	1½ cups Wine Vinegar.
1 Blade of Mace.	½ cup Water.

A Shredded Onion (optional).

Clean, bone, and fillet the herring. Sprinkle with salt, and mill fresh black pepper over them. Roll up tightly from tail to head and pack into a pie-dish or shallow casserole. Distribute the spices among the fish, and add the onion if desired. Pour over the herring just enough vinegar and water to cover. Place a grease-proof paper over the dish, and bake in a slow oven for 1½ hours.

FINNAN-HADDIE
(FISHERWIFE'S FASHION)

1 Smoked Haddock.	1 teaspoonful Cornflour.
1 oz. Butter.	Pepper.

1 cup Milk.

Skin a good-sized fish* and cut into neat pieces. Melt the butter in a saucepan, put in the fish, sprinkle with pepper, cover closely, and cook gently for five minutes. Break the cornflour in a little milk, add the rest of the milk, pour over the fish, and cook gently for another five minutes. Take out the fish, arrange in a shallow dish, and pour the sauce over.

A poached egg or a daub of whipped cream may be served on each portion of fish.

Lightly smoked haddocks, such as the pale Moray Firths, are excellent cut up and fried with bacon.

* To skin a haddock, hold the skin side to the fire (or place under the grill) for a minute or two ; then lay it on the palm of one hand and clap it with the other. Begin at the head, and the skin should come off quite easily.

CREAMED FINNAN-HADDIE

1 **Smoked Haddock.**	**2 oz. Grated Cheese.**
½ **pint White Sauce.**	**A pinch of Mustard.**
	1 oz. Butter.

Cook the haddock in just enough water to cover. Remove skin and bone, and cut the fish into small neat pieces. Grease a shallow fireproof dish and lay the fish in it. Make a good white sauce—half a pint or more according to the size of the fish, using some of the liquor from the fish; when well cooked, add the cheese with pepper and mustard, but no salt, as the fish will probably be salt enough. Stir until the cheese is melted, but do not re-cook the sauce. Pour the sauce over the haddock, sprinkle with grated cheese, dot with butter, make thoroughly hot, and place under the grill to brown.

BLAWN WHITINGS

The age-old method of our fisherfolk to give *goût* to white fish, which is apt to be very insipid, is to give them a touch of the elements principally the wind and the sun. Hence our " blawn " or wind-blown whitings, which M. Soyer has described as " the most light, wholesome, and delicious food that could be served for breakfast "; our " rizzared " or sun-dried haddocks; and our once famous " cabbie-claw." Skate, again, used to be laid for a day or two on the grass, with a grassy sod over it (grass side down) or alternatively, " rizzared."

Choose perfectly fresh fish, and gut and clean them without delay; then skin (unless very small), and remove the eyes. Cover them with salt, rubbing it well in along the bone from which the guts have been removed; then shake off the superfluous salt, pass a string through the eye-holes, and hang them up either outside in a fresh, cool breeze but out of the sun, or inside in a passage where there is a current of air. Take down and cook for breakfast next morning, or, if large, leave until the following or even the third morning. Roll lightly in flour, and broil gently over a slow fire. Serve very hot, with a pat of butter rubbed over each.

RIZZARED HADDIES

Fresh Haddocks. **Salt.** **Butter.**

Choose perfectly fresh fish, preferably of medium size ; gut, wipe, and leave in salt overnight. String on a thick wire passed through the eye-holes, and hang them on a wall in the open air, but be careful not to expose them to the *direct* rays of the sun. Leave them for two or three days, then take them down, skin them, remove the backbone, broil on a gridiron, rub with butter, and serve.

Failing a gridiron, they may be cooked under the grill.

CABBIE-CLAW

A Fresh Cod (2-3 lbs.) **Parsley.**
I pint Egg Sauce. **Salt.**
Horse Radish **Pepper.**

The fish must be perfectly fresh. Clean, skin, and wipe it ; take out the eyes ; sprinkle it, inside and out, with salt, rubbing it well in along the bone from which the guts have been removed, and let it lie overnight. Next morning hang it out in the open air, preferably in a breeze, but always out of the sun's rays. Leave for forty-eight hours or longer, according to the degree of " highness " desired. Put on in boiling water with a few sprigs of parsley and some scraped horse radish, and cook gently till tender. Remove the skin and bone and cut the fish into small neat pieces, or flake if desired. Place it in a shallow dish—if liked, within a border of mashed potato—and pour the egg sauce over. Garnish with red pepper and chopped parsley.

The egg sauce may be made with half milk and half fish-bree.

CRAPPIT HEIDS
(STUFFED HADDOCK HEADS)

4 Haddock Heads. **Salt.**
4 Haddock Livers. **Pepper.**
Oatmeal. **A little Milk.**

Chop the livers, which must be perfectly fresh, and mix them with an equal quantity of oatmeal. Season with salt and pepper, and bind with milk. Stuff the heads with this mixture. If preferred, they may be stuffed with Slot, Stap, or Roe Crappin.

27

Put the crappit or stuffed haddocks on end in a buttered stew-pan, pour over some fish stock, and boil them gently for half an hour.

A " haddock lug " (the flesh behind the " ear ") has always been considered a tit-bit.

A more sophisticated stuffing can be made with some minced lobster or crab, a boned anchovy, a grated egg-yolk, a few breadcrumbs, salt, white pepper, and cayenne, and some dots of butter, with beaten egg and, if liked, a little oyster liquor to bind.

TO BOIL SALMON
(PLAIN SCOTS STYLE)

Salmon.　　　　　**Salt.**　　　　　**Water.**

Scale and clean the fish without any unnecessary washing or handling. Place it on the strainer and in a roomy fish-kettle, and pour in sufficient cold spring water amply to cover the fish. (If only a piece is used, put on in warm water.) Bring slowly to the boil, skim carefully, add salt (half an ounce to a quart of water), cover, and simmer gently for the required time. (Allow roughly ten minutes to the pound and ten minutes over, but use your eyes.) As soon as it is done, lift up the strainer and rest it across the pan to drain the fish, throwing a soft cloth or flannel in several folds over it. Serve with fresh green peas, mealy potatoes, pepper and vinegar, and no other sauce than a little of the salmon bree.

The carver should help a slice of the thick part with a smaller slice of the thin, which is preferred by the discriminating.

Cold, the fish is best served as salmon mayonnaise.

A slice of salmon should preferably not be boiled, but cooked slowly in its own steam and juices in a buttered soup-plate, with a sprinkling of salt, over a pan of boiling water with a cover over the fish. The time varies according to the thickness.

TO BROIL SALMON STEAKS

Salmon.　　　　　**Salt.**
Butter.　　　　　**Pepper.**

Cut steaks about an inch thick from thickest part of the fish. Season. Butter pieces of white paper, fold the steak in them, twist the ends, and broil over a slow fire for ten to twelve minutes, turning them over frequently till done.

Remove the paper, place a very thin slice of butter on each steak, garnish with horseradish or fried parsley, and serve very hot.

A lobster or shrimp sauce is sometimes served with the steaks.

SALMON SEALS

½ lb. Boiled Salmon.	Salt and Pepper.
1½ lbs. Potatoes.	A little Beaten Egg.
1 or 2 Eggs.	A few Breadcrumbs.
A walnut of Butter.	Dripping to fry.

Boil the potatoes and mash with a little butter and pepper ; then form into small round cakes about a quarter-inch thick. Hard-boil one or two eggs and chop small. Flake the salmon and mix with the egg. Season with salt and pepper. Press a spoonful of the mixture into a potato cake and put another cake over it. When all are ready, egg and breadcrumb them, and fry in hot dripping to a golden brown.

This method makes a little salmon go a long way.

TO FRY SILLOCKS

Sillocks (Saith in their first season).	**Butter.**
Oatmeal.	**Salt.**

" The perfect dish of sillocks must be caught and cooked by the consumers.

"When the moon rises on a late summer's night, you must fish far out on a sea moved only by the slow, broad Atlantic swell. And the little mountain of sillocks, the reward of cold but exciting hours, must be ' dite ' in a moonlit rockpool. Then home at cockcrow.

" Around the kitchen fire, while the rest of the household sleep, come the happy rites of cooking and eating.

" Each tiny, headless fish, wrapped in a stout jacket of salted oatmeal, is popped into a pan of hot butter. There they bounce and spit while the fishers, ringed round pan and fire, exquisitely thaw. At last, richly brown and curled into fantastic shapes, and so tender they almost fall to pieces, they are dished.

"Sillock-eating at the kitchen table dispenses with knives and forks. You lift a sillock gently between thumb and forefinger, snip off the tail, press the plump sides—and the backbone shoots forth! The delicious morsel left—hot, crisp oatmeal and sweet melting fish—you eat on buttered 'bere' bread, a darkly brown, flatly sour scone."

Note.—This recipe for a favourite Orkney and Shetland dish won a prize some years ago in a competition in *Everyman*.

TO BROIL TROUT

Trout.	Salt.
Butter.	Pepper.

Trout is greatly improved if slightly salted and allowed to lie overnight. In the morning wipe the fish, split open, and remove the bone. Brush with melted butter, season with salt and pepper, lay on a hot gridiron, and cook on each side for five-ten minutes, according to the thickness of the fish. Or cook under the grill.

Serve with lemon and watercress.

TO FRY TROUT
(SCOTS STYLE)

Trout.	Salt.	Milk.
Oatmeal.	Pepper.	Lard.

Prepare as above. In the morning, wipe the fish, dip in milk, and coat thickly with coarse oatmeal. Place in a pan of smoking hot lard and cook very quickly for a few minutes, until the fish are browned on both sides. Drain and serve.

With butter and lemon, this makes a succulent breakfast dish.

POTTED TROUT

Trout.	Pepper.
Butter.	Salt.

Fry the fish in the ordinary way. While still warm, lift the flesh in sections from the bones, and place each section lengthwise in a buttered pie-dish. Sprinkle each layer with salt and pepper, and run melted butter over the whole.

To be eaten cold.

BUTTERED TROUT

Trout.	**Salt.**
Butter.	**Pepper.**
Flour.	**Lemon.**

Cut off the fins, and clean and wipe the fish. Sprinkle with salt and pepper, and roll in flour. Melt a good piece of butter in a shallow pan or a fireproof dish, put in the trout, and brown on both sides, basting frequently. When cooked, remove to a hot ashet ; then squeeze a little lemon juice into the butter in the pan and pour over the fish.

FISH CUSTARD

4 Fillets of White Fish	**I Egg.**
Salt.	**I teacupful Milk.**
White Pepper.	**Squeeze of Lemon.**

Sole or haddock is best for this dish. Season the fillets and roll up neatly, skin side innermost. Arrange in a buttered pie-dish. Beat the egg lightly, mix with the milk, add a few grains of salt and pepper and a very little lemon juice, and pour over the fish. Bake in a rather slow oven for forty-five minutes or until the custard is set.

FISH BALLER

I cupful Flaked White Fish.	**2 teaspoonfuls Minced Parsley.**
I cupful Shelled Shrimps.	**½ teaspoonful Powdered Thyme.**
I cupful Breadcrumbs, fine.	**I Egg.**
Salt and Pepper.	**Egg-yolk and Crumbs (to coat).**

Pass the cooked fish and shrimps twice through the mincer. Put into a wooden bowl with the other dry ingredients, add the well-beaten egg, mix thoroughly, and pound with a potato masher for twenty minutes or till smooth. Form into small balls—these may be slightly flattened if desired—and coat with beaten egg-yolk and crumbs. Fry for a minute in deep fat (390 F.).

PARTAN PIE

I large Partan (Crab).	Salt and Pepper.
A walnut of Butter.	A pinch of Grated Nutmeg.
I tablespoonful Breadcrumbs.	2-3 tablespoonfuls Wine Vinegar
I teaspoonful Made Mustard.	or Lemon Juice.

Boil your crab and leave it to cool. Remove all the meat from the claws and body (discarding the " apron " and gills), put it into a small bowl and chop it up. Season with salt, pepper, and nutmeg, and add the breadcrumbs, vinegar and mustard. Add some tiny bits of fresh butter, and beat all well together. Wash the shell and polish with a little salad oil, and refill with the mixture. If to be eaten hot, brown under the grill. (The old cottage way was to heat a shovel in the fire and hold it over the pie.) If preferred cold, garnish with red pepper and chopped parsley.

FISHERMAN'S PIE

I lb. Boiled Salt Cod.*	I dessertspoonful Chopped Parsley.
I lb. Mashed Potatoes.	I dessertspoonful Butter.
I Hard-boiled Egg.	½ teaspoonful Made Mustard.
I Shallot or	Black Pepper.
a few Chives.	Milk to moisten.

Flake the fish and mix with the hot mashed potatoes. Chop the egg and the shallot or chives, and add these with the parsley. Add the butter broken up, and the milk made hot. Mix thoroughly, season with black pepper and the mustard (the latter moistened preferably with vinegar), and see that it is salt enough. Turn into a buttered pie-dish, dot with butter or margarine, and brown in a good oven.

The egg may be omitted, and the dish served with egg-sauce.

Parsnips go particularly well with dried cod.

* The fish should be soaked in lukewarm water for from two to twelve hours, or longer if very salt, the water being changed two or three times. It is then put on in cold water and boiled for 20-30 minutes, or till the flesh comes away easily from the bones.

MEAT

ORMIDALE STEAK PIE

1¼ lbs. Beef Steak.	1 teaspoonful Worcester Sauce.
¼ lb. Kidney.	1 teaspoonful Tomato Sauce.
1 Onion (optional).	1 teaspoonful Vinegar.
1 tablespoonful Flour.	½ pint Water.
1 teaspoonful Salt.	½ lb. Flaky Pastry.
¼ teaspoonful Pepper.	Milk *or* Beaten Egg to glaze.

Remove the fat from the steak and cut the lean meat into ¾-inch cubes. Prepare the kidneys and cut into tiny cubes. Dip each piece in the flour. Melt the fat removed from the steak. Mince and add the onion, and fry gently for a few minutes ; then put in the steak and kidney and stir constantly until the surface is well seared and browned. Remove to a stew-pan. Add the boiling water to the remaining fat, and strain. Add to this the salt and pepper, sauces, and vinegar, and pour over the meat. Cover tightly, and cook over a low heat until the meat is tender. Turn the meat into a pie-dish with a half-inch rim. It should be filled to the brim. Place a china funnel (or small earthen teacup turned upside down) in the middle, and leave the meat to get quite cold. Meanwhile strain off the gravy in the pan and thicken with a little flour. (A little butter may also be added.) Pour half of it over the meat. Cover with pastry, leaving a hole in the centre for the steam to escape ; decorate, and brush with milk or beaten egg. Bake in a good oven for thirty minutes. Re-heat the rest of the gravy and pour into the pie through the funnel just before serving.

C

MUSSELBURGH PIE

1 lb. Steak.	1 oz. Flour.
1 dozen Oysters.	Salt and Pepper.
1 or 2 Shallots.	Few grains Cayenne.
Small piece Suet *or*	1½ gills Water *or* Stock.
Bacon Fat.	½ lb. Rough Puff Pastry.

Beat the steak and cut into thin strips. Beard the oysters, then halve them and wrap each half, together with a scrap of fat, in a strip of meat. Season flour with salt, pepper, and cayenne, dip each roll in this and pack neatly in a pie-dish round a china funnel. Add the water, cover with the pastry, trim, and decorate; brush with milk or beaten egg, and bake in an oven (pretty hot at first, then moderate) for 1½ hours.

MINCE

1 lb. Stewing Steak.	1 Onion.
2 tablespoonfuls Gravy	Salt and Pepper.
or Water.	Butter *or* Dripping.

Remove all skin and gristle and all but a little of the fat from the meat. If minced at home, remove all juice that comes from it. This may make the dish sufficiently moist without adding water. If bought minced, add later two tablespoonfuls of pure gravy run from roast beef; or add water; but don't use stock. Put the mince into a buttered stew-pan, and beat well with a wooden spoon, and stir to prevent knots. When the pink colour has disappeared, but not before, add salt, pepper, the hot gravy or water, and a whole peeled raw onion. Put the lid on, draw to the side, and simmer for thirty-forty minutes, stirring occasionally.

The mince may also be cooked in a covered stone jar in the oven, but will take longer.

Barley, oatmeal, or breadcrumbs are often added for reasons of economy.

The better the quality of the steak, the better the mince.

HIKERS' HOT POT

1 lb. Hough.	1 Apple.
½ lb. Pork Sausages.	1 Onion.
½ lb. Tomatoes.	1 oz. Flour.
1 lb. Potatoes.	Salt and Pepper.

Cut the meat up neatly into small pieces. Skin the sausages and cut each into three or four pieces. Dip the meat and sausage in seasoned flour. Peel and slice the potatoes, apple, and onion. Slice the tomatoes. Arrange in layers in an earthenware casserole, beginning with potatoes, then adding hough and sausage, then the apple, onion, and tomato mixed. Finish with a layer of potato. Fill the casserole one-third full with stock or water, and cook in a moderate oven for two hours.

WHITE COLLOPS

Veal.	Lemon Rind.
Flour.	Mushroom Ketchup.
Salt and Pepper.	Butter.
Mace.	Stock.

Cut the veal into half-inch slices or collops, beat with a rolling pin, sprinkle with salt and pepper, and dip in flour. Melt a little butter in a stew-pan, put in the collops, and brown them nicely. Surround with veal or other stock, cover closely, and cook slowly till tender. When nearly ready, add a little grated lemon rind and a flavouring of mushroom ketchup, with a little mace, and any more salt and pepper required. Thicken the sauce and strain over the meat.

The dish may be garnished with curled rashers of toasted bacon. In the old days oysters and mushrooms were used.

MUTTON-HAM

A Gigot of Mutton (c. 14 lbs.).	2 oz. Brown Sugar.
	½ oz. Saltpetre.
1 lb. Common Salt.	

Trim the gigot and rub all over with the sugar. Let it lie for an hour, then rub in the saltpetre, and finally the salt, thrusting some with your finger down the hole in the shank. Let it lie in pickle for three weeks (more or less), keeping it carefully covered with a cloth, and basting it with the brine every other day. Then take it out and press it with a weight for one day. It may now be smoked for ten or fifteen days, or hung up to dry in the kitchen.

In the Highlands, mutton hams are smoked over juniper twigs, or alternatively, a handful or two of juniper berries are scattered over the smouldering oak sawdust.

The ham is sometimes spiced as follows :—

Mix together 1 lb. common salt, 1 oz. saltpetre, 4 oz. brown sugar, 1 oz. black pepper, 1 oz. Jamaica pepper, and ½ oz. coriander seeds, and rub the gigot thoroughly with these. Let it lie for two weeks in the trough, basting and finishing as above.

If the ham is to be boiled soon after it is smoked, soak it for one hour ; otherwise it may need several hours. Put on in cold water, bring to the boil, and cook gently for two hours. It is eaten cold at breakfast, lunch, or supper.

HAGGIS
(TRADITIONAL BUT-AND-BEN RECIPE)

1 Sheep's Pluck:	**1 breakfastcupful Fine Oatmeal.**
Liver, Lights, and Heart.	**2 or 3 Onions.**
The Large Stomach Bag.	**Salt and Pepper.**
½ lb. Fresh Beef Suet.	**Pinch of Cayenne.**
1 breakfastcupful Stock or Gravy.	

Clean the paunch or stomach bag thoroughly; wash first in cold water, then plunge into boiling water and scrape; then leave to soak overnight in cold salted water. In the morning put it aside with the rough side turned out. Wash the small bag and the pluck, and put them on to boil in cold water to cover, letting the wind-pipe hang out over the pot to let any impurities pass out freely. Boil for an hour and a half, then remove and cut away the pipes and any superfluities of gristle. Mince the heart and lights, and grate half the liver. (The rest is not required.) Mince the onions and suet, and toast the oatmeal very slowly before the fire or in a warm oven. Mix all these ingredients together and season with salt, plenty of black pepper, and a pinch of cayenne. Pour over this sufficient of the pluck bree to make the mixture sappy. Fill the bag rather more than half full—say five-eighths. It needs plenty of room to swell. Press out the air and sew the bag up securely. Put it into a pot of fast-boiling water, and prick it with a large needle when it first swells, to prevent bursting. Boil slowly but steadily for three hours, without the lid, adding more boiling water as required. Serve very hot without any garnish.

At a Burns Supper the haggis is usually piped in and is served with " neeps " and " nips "—mashed turnips and " nips " of whisky—and, of course, potatoes.

POT HAGGIS

½ lb. Liver.	1 cup Oatmeal.
¼ lb. Beef Suet.	1 cup Liver Bree.
1-2 Onions.	Salt and Pepper.

Boil the liver for forty minutes ; cool ; then grate or pass through the mincer. Parboil the onions at the same time, then chop them small. Chop the suet. Put the oatmeal in a thick-bottomed dry pan, and toss over the fire till lightly browned. Add the liver, suet, and onions, and season with salt and freshly milled black pepper. Moisten with the bree or liquor in which the liver was boiled. Turn into a greased bowl, cover with a greased paper, and steam for two hours.

The haggis may be covered with a lid of suet pastry before it is steamed.

FRIED STEAK AND ONIONS
(FARMHOUSE STYLE)

Steak.	Butter.
Onions.	Salt and Butter.

The steak should be cut more thinly than for grilling. To prepare it, lay it on a mincing-board, and with a knife cut across the skin-covered edge all the way round as far as the skin goes, the cuts being about an inch apart. (This prevents the skin from shrinking and the steak from curling up, and thus the meat is better cooked.) Then beat the steak with a rolling-pin to make it tender.

Melt an ounce or so of salt butter in a clean frying-pan, and when sizzling hot (but not burnt) put in the steak. Turn, and keep turning every minute or so until it is nicely browned ; then lift it to the side of the fire and cook gently for ten minutes. Then turn, put on the fire again, and cook for five minutes longer. Butter a hot ashet, sprinkle with a very little salt and white pepper, and dish the steak on this. Cover with onions fried as follows, and send hot to table.

Have ready a plateful of onions sliced very thin, and sprinkled with salt and pepper. Put them into a frying-pan in which you have melted some butter or dripping, lay a dish over them to keep in the steam, and turn them about until they are thoroughly cooked, allowing them plenty of time. They should be soft and brown. Serve very hot.

POTTED HOUGH

3 lbs. Hough (Shin of Beef).   **Salt and Pepper.**
1 Nap Bone.   **Water.**

Put hough and bone into a pot, cover with cold water, and add salt. Bring very slowly to boiling-point, and simmer very gently for five or six hours until the meat is loosed from the bones. Remove the bones, chop the meat small or mince it, and return to the pot with the stock; add a little more boiling water if necessary, season with salt and pepper, and boil for another ten minutes—no longer. When cool, turn into wetted moulds.

It is an excellent plan to put the hough on the fire at night, bring it almost to boiling-point, then place it on the hob and let it simmer very gently all night, without letting it boil. Prepared thus, it has a richer taste than when cooked in the ordinary way.

If liked slightly spiced, tie a half-teaspoonful apiece of whole spices, whole mace, and peppercorns in muslin, and add when the meat first comes to the boil. Remove when sufficiently seasoned

SHEEP'S HEAD BRAWN

A Sheep's Head.   **Salt.**
½ lb. Bacon.   **Pepper.**

Boil a sheep's head for three hours or longer, as for Pow-sowdie, and boil the bacon with it for half an hour or till tender. When cooked, remove the flesh, skin the tongue, and pass them, together with the bacon, through the mincer. Season well, and press into a basin. Put a plate over it, and place a weight on the plate. Turn out when cold, and serve with salad.

AYRSHIRE GALANTINE

1 lb. Ayrshire Bacon.	¼ teaspoonful Grated Nutmeg.
1 lb. Beef Steak.	¼ teaspoonful Ground Mace.
½ lb. Breadcrumbs.	Pinch of Black Pepper.
½ teaspoonful Salt.	2 Eggs.

A little Stock or Water.

Remove all skin and gristle from the beef and bacon ; then mince and weigh. Place in a basin, and stir in the crumbs, salt, and spices. Beat the eggs and add, together with sufficient stock to moisten the mixture. Turn on to a lightly floured board and shape into a roll. Tie securely in a floured pudding cloth. (It is advisable to sew the edges together.) Place in a pan half full of boiling stock or water, with some pieces of carrot, turnip, onion, and one or two sprigs of parsley. Cover, and simmer gently for two hours. Remove the galantine, and if the cloth has become loose, re-tie it firmly. Place on an ashet with another on top, and weight it down. Leave till next day ; then remove the weights and cloth, brush with glaze, and serve when the glaze is set.

SMALL MUTTON PIES

12 oz. Lean Mutton.	Salt and Pepper.
1 Shallot.	1-2 tablespoonfuls Stock
1 teaspoonful Minced Parsley.	or Water.
½ teaspoonful Thyme.	2 teaspoonfuls Worcester
2 or 3 Mushrooms (optional).	Sauce.

HOT-WATER CRUST

1 lb. Flour.	½ teaspoonful Salt.
4 oz. Fresh Beef Dripping.	½ pint Water.

Remove skin, bone, and gristle from the mutton and chop small. Peel and chop the mushrooms, if used, and the shallot. Mix these with the parsley, thyme, salt, and pepper, and set aside.

To make the crust, sieve the flour into a bowl, and add the salt. Put the dripping and water into a saucepan and bring to the boil ; then pour immediately into a well in the flour. Mix at first with a spoon or knife, but when cool enough use the hands, and mix quickly into one lump. Turn on to a floured board, and knead lightly till free from cracks.

Put aside about a third of the paste to keep warm, and divide the rest into six pieces. With these line six small ring tins, or mould them into small cases round a tumbler. Fill the cases with the mutton mixture, and just moisten with the stock or water. Cut rounds from the remainder of the paste, moisten the edges, and cover the pies, pressing the edges of paste firmly together. Trim with a pair of scissors, make a hole in the centre of each pie, and brush with a little milk or beaten egg. Bake for thirty-forty minutes in a moderate oven. Remove the pies from the tins, fill them up with hot gravy or stock flavoured with Worcester sauce or ketchup, and serve piping hot.

FORFAR BRIDIES

1 lb. Beefsteak.	Salt.
3 oz. Suet.	Pepper.
1 Onion.	Flour.
Water.	

Beat the steak with a rolling-pin, then cut it into narrow strips, and cut these across into one-inch lengths. Season with pepper and salt, and divide into three portions. Mince the suet and the onion. Make a stiff dough with flour, water, and a seasoning of salt; roll out very thin, and cut into three ovals. Cover half of each oval with the meat, leaving a narrow margin round the edge. Sprinkle the suet and the onion over the meat; wet the edges of the pastry, fold over, and crimp with finger and thumb. Nip a small hole on the top of each, and bake for about half an hour in a quick oven.

Short or rough puff pastry may be used for bridies.

GLASGOW TRIPE

Tripe.	A Marrow Bone *or*
Salt and Pepper.	A Knuckle of Veal.

Clean and blanch the tripe, and cut into broad strips. Season, roll up neatly, secure with a thread, and place in a stoneware jar along with the bone or knuckle. Cover closely, and place in a pot of water. Boil for eight or ten hours or longer, filling up the pot as the water boils away.

Keep the tripe in its own jelly, and use as required. It may be re-heated in onion sauce or tomato sauce, or fried in batter, or (as some prefer it), eaten cold.

GAME AND POULTRY

ROAST HAUNCH OF VENISON

Venison varies greatly in quality. The high ground in summer, it is said, gives the sweetest pickings, and stags that dwell habitually among the stony tops make incomparably the best venison.

A Haunch of Venison.	**Gravy (additional).**
Paste of Flour and Water.	**Port Wine** *or*
Salt.	**Walnut Ketchup** *or*
Butter.	**Shallot Vinegar.**
Flour.	**Rowan Jelly.**

The venison must, of course, be well hung. The essential thing is to counteract its dryness. When to be cooked, sponge it with lukewarm water and rub with butter or lard. Cover with sheets of paper, well greased or steeped in salad oil, and over this lay a paste of flour and water ½-inch thick. Swathe with strong paper again, secure with greased string, and drench the whole in melted butter or other fat to prevent the paper from catching fire. Roast for three or four hours or longer, according to the age and size of the haunch. Half an hour before it ought to be done, remove the swathings and test with a skewer. Season with salt, dredge with flour, baste well with melted butter (in more spacious days it was claret and butter), and brown as quickly as possible. Remove to a very hot ashet and pour over it a little hot gravy flavoured with a glass of port wine. Celerity in sending from fire to table is everything. Serve with rowan or other sharp-flavoured jelly.

" With venison," says a Scottish gourmet, " Burgundy goes as naturally as iced punch with the turtle, and for more obvious reason. The bouquet of the one and the savour of the other were evidently destined to make a happy love-match."

VENISON PASTY

1½ lbs. Breast *or* Shoulder of Venison.	Powdered Allspice.
⅓ pint Mutton Gravy.	Salt.
Black Pepper.	Walnut Pickle *or* Port Wine.

Rough Puff Pastry.

The meat should be well hung. Remove the bone, lay the meat flat on the table, and beat all over with a rolling-pin. Sprinkle with salt, black pepper, and allspice, and place on it a few pieces of tender mutton fat that have been cooked and allowed to get cold. Roll up the meat and tie securely in three places. Sprinkle with more salt, pepper, and allspice, and put into a stew-pan with the gravy. Cover closely, bring slowly to the boil, and simmer very gently for four hours. Remove the tapes, and leave overnight in a cold place. Next day remove the cake of fat on the gravy, cut up the meat in suitable pieces, and fill the pie-dish, placing a funnel in the centre. Add some of the gravy, to which a tablespoonful of port wine or a little walnut pickle may be added, cover with pastry, and bake until the crust is cooked (about half an hour). Re-heat the remainder of the gravy and pour into the pie through the funnel just before serving.

The venison roll may be served as it is, hot from the stew-pan, with rowan jelly as an accompaniment.

GILLIE'S VENISON
(HIGHLANDS)

Venison.	Flour.
Bacon Fat *or* Beef Dripping.	Salt.
	Pepper.

This is perhaps the simplest and certainly (say the gillies) the best way of cooking venison.

Cut the meat into cubes — say ¾ - inch — and dip in seasoned flour. Melt plenty of fat in a strong iron pot—two inches is a good depth—put in the venison, and keep turning till browned all over. Sprinkle with salt and pepper, cover closely, and cook gently for an hour or until the meat is tender. Dish the meat, pour off any superfluous fat, and make gravy in the usual way, thickening it with flour.

This basic recipe may be varied in several ways. A chopped

onion may be browned in the fat before the venison is put in. A rasher or two of bacon may be cut into short lengths and added. Jamaica pepper and a clove or two will give it more *goût*. A few chestnuts, peeled and scraped, may be cooked with the meat. And the laird adds a glass of port wine.

Serve the stew with mealy potatoes. Celery, with its nutty flavour, makes an excellent accompaniment to venison or any game.

ROAST GROUSE
(HIGHLAND FASHION)

Grouse.	**Butter** or **Bacon Fat.**
Rashers of Bacon.	**Salt and Pepper.**
Lemon or **Red Whortle-**	**Cayenne.**
berries or **Cranberries.**	**Toast.**

Of all varieties of feathered game, the red grouse, which is peculiar to Scotland and the North of England, has the most exquisite flavour. It should hang for from three to ten days, according to its age and the weather. Only young birds should be roasted.

The essential thing is to avoid dryness. When ready to cook, the birds should be carefully plucked to avoid breaking the delicate skin, and wiped (not washed) inside and out with a damp cloth. Put into each bird (but not into the crop) an ounce or two of bacon fat, or of butter into which you have worked a little lemon juice, pepper, and salt. Red whortle-berries or cranberries may be used instead, as they bring out the flavour and keep them as moist as butter does. Wrap the birds in generous rashers of fat bacon and then in greaseproof paper. A sprig or two of heather is sometimes enclosed. (Heather has a marked affinity with the peat and ling-scented flesh of the grouse.) Place them, breast down, on a trivet in the roasting-tin, and put them into a good oven. Grouse should be neither over- nor under-done. They require from twenty-five to thirty-five minutes according to their size. Ten minutes before serving remove the wrappings, flour the birds, and brown them.

Meanwhile boil the livers for ten minutes and pound them in a mortar with a little butter, salt, and cayenne, then spread

43

on pieces of toast large enough to hold a bird. Place the toast under the birds (but not in the fat in the pan to get sodden) and leave during the last few minutes of the roasting.

The usual accompaniments are fried breadcrumbs, fried oatmeal, or skirlie; chip potatoes, watercress, French beans, and clear gravy. Cranberry or rowan jelly goes well with grouse, and there are some who swear by pickled peaches.

STOVED GROUSE
(ARGYLL)

Melt a teaspoonful of sugar in a frying-pan, add a table-spoonful of bacon fat, and brown the grouse well in this, turning it over frequently. Heat some bacon fat in a small casserole with a closely fitting lid. Put in the bird, cover, and cook on the top of the range for 1½ hours, turning it over frequently.

Raw chipped potatoes, sprinkled with salt, may be added about half an hour before the grouse is ready.

HIGHLAND HOTPOT

1 **Brace of Grouse.**	4 **medium Potatoes.**
1 **small Rabbit.**	**Black Pepper.**
¼ **lb. Streaky Bacon.**	**Allspice.**
Small Head of Celery.	**Salt.**
½ **Small White Cabbage.**	**Mushroom Ketchup** or
4 **small Onions.**	**Red Wine.**
Stock or **Water.**	

Prepare the grouse (as for roasting) and the rabbit, and cut into joints. Divide the rashers into two or three pieces. The joints may be dipped in seasoned flour and browned in the frying-pan, but this is not necessary. Prepare and slice the celery, onions, and potatoes, and arrange with the grouse and rabbit in layers in an earthenware casserole. Fill about one-third full with stock or water. Bring to the boil, then add the cabbage, seasonings, and the mushroom ketchup or wine. Cover and cook in a moderate oven for 2-2½ hours.

HIGHLAND HARE CAKES

½ lb. Hare.	½ teaspoonful Celery Salt.
¼ lb. Fat Pork.	¼ teaspoonful Paprika.
½ Small Onion.	1 teaspoonful Mushroom
2 oz. Stale Bread.	Ketchup.
Salt.	1 Egg.

This is a good way of using up the unused meat from the hare when making hare soup.

Mince the hare and pork together, and mix thoroughly. Soak the bread in cold water till soft, then squeeze out the water and mix the pulp with meat. Chop the onion, fry it lightly, and add with the other seasonings. Mix well, and bind with the beaten egg. Shape into cakes 1¼ inches thick, coat with crumbs, and fry in hot fat till well browned on both sides.

These cakes are improved by placing on each a pat of seasoned butter (two ounces of butter creamed with half teaspoonful salt and a few grains of pepper). Serve with grilled tomatoes and creamed potatoes.

KINGDOM OF FIFE PIE

1 large Rabbit or	Forcemeat:
2 small ones.	1 Rabbit Liver.
1 lb. Pickled Pork.	1 Rasher Fat Bacon.
1 Egg (optional).	4 oz. Breadcrumbs.
Grated Nutmeg.	1 tablespoonful Parsley.
Salt and Pepper.	1 tablespoonful Dried Thyme.
1 gill Stock or	A little Grated Lemon Rind.
Gravy.	A pinch Grated Nutmeg.
Forcemeat Balls.	Salt and Pepper.
Rough Puff Pastry.	Egg or Milk to bind.

Skin the rabbit, cut it into joints, and let it lie for an hour in cold water. Make a gravy with the carcase and liver, removing the liver when cooked. Slice the pork, and season with salt, pepper, and nutmeg. Make forcemeat balls as below. Hard-boil and slice the egg. Pack rabbit, pork, balls, and egg into a pie-dish, and add a gill of the gravy. Cover with rough puff pastry. It is advisable to make three holes in the paste, as a rabbit pie needs plenty of ventilation. Put into a hot oven, but lower the heat presently and cook in a very moderate oven for 2½ hours. When cooked, pour in another gill of gravy or good seasoned stock. If the pie is to be served cold, a little gelatine may be dissolved in the gravy.

For the forcemeat, chop liver and bacon, mix with dry ingredients, bind with egg or milk, and form into balls.

CHICKEN STOVIES
(HIGHLANDS)

1 Chicken *or* Fowl.	Salt.
2 lbs. Potatoes.	Pepper.
2 Onions.	Butter.
3 gills Water.	

Prepare the bird and cut into pieces for serving. Cut up the potatoes roughly, and slice the onions. Arrange alternate layers of chicken, potatoes, and onions in a casserole, sprinkling each layer with salt and pepper, and dotting with butter. Pour in the water and cover tightly. Cook for three-four hours in a slow oven. Or cook in an iron pot over a gentle heat.

MINCE-FOWL

2 cups Cooked and Diced Fowl.	Pinch of Grated Nutmeg.
½ cup Minced Mushrooms.	1 dessertspoon Chopped Parsley.
3 oz. Butter.	1 dessertspoon Chopped Chives.
2 oz. Flour.	Few drops Lemon Juice.
Salt and Pepper.	1 cup Chicken Stock.
2 tablespoons Cream (optional).	

Stew the mushrooms, covered, in half the butter for fifteen minutes. Melt the remainder of the butter, add the flour, stir till smooth, gradually stir in the stock and cook, still stirring, for ten minutes. Season. Add the diced fowl (preferably the breast), the mushrooms with the butter in which they were cooked, nutmeg, parsley, chives, lemon juice and cream. Make very hot and serve with a border of mashed potatoes or of rice boiled in chicken stock, or with scrambled eggs.

VEGETABLES AND SALADS

STOVIES
(STOVED POTATOES)

Potatoes.   **Salt.**
Butter.   **Water.**

Choose potatoes of good quality. Peel them, and put them on with just enough water to cover the bottom of the pan and prevent burning. Sprinkle with salt and put tiny bits of butter here and there. Cover closely, and simmer very gently till soft and melted.

Dripping may be used in place of butter, and sliced onions (first tossed in the dripping) may be added, with a seasoning of pepper; but the dish is best prepared as above.

COLCANNON

Potatoes.   **Butter** *or* **Dripping.**
Cabbage.   **Salt and Pepper.**

Take equal quantities of boiled potatoes and boiled cabbage. Mash the potatoes and mince the cabbage. Melt a piece of butter or dripping in a saucepan, allowing approximately one ounce to one pound vegetables. Put in the potatoes and cabbage, and salt and pepper to taste, mix well, make thoroughly hot, and serve.

The mixture may be turned into a greased pie-dish, sprinkled with grated cheese, dotted with butter or margarine, and browned in a hot oven.

CLAPSHOT
(ORKNEY)

Potatoes.	Salt.
Turnips.	Pepper.
Chives *or* Shallot.	Butter *or* Dripping.

Boil, drain, and dry equal quantities of potatoes and turnip. Chop the chives or shallot. Break up a good piece of dripping. Mash the potatoes and turnips well together with the dripping. Sprinkle with the chives, season well, mix thoroughly, and serve very hot.

LANG KAIL

Green Kail.	Salt and Pepper.
Butter.	Water.

Take two or three stalks of fresh crisp young green kail, separate the blades from the stalk, wash well, and boil till tender in salted water. Drain carefully, and beat up the blades with butter. Season with salt and pepper.

Serve with fresh pork or other meat.

BUTTERED PEAS

Peas.	Butter.	Pepper.
Mint.	Salt.	Sugar.

Use only young tender green peas for this dish. The smaller the sweeter. Melt a good piece of butter in a saucepan, put in the peas, add a sprig or two of mint, cover, and cook slowly over a gentle heat for about an hour, shaking occasionally. When half cooked, add a sprinkling of salt and pepper and a very little sifted sugar. Remove the mint, and serve very hot.

ARRAN POTATO SALAD

10-12 Potatoes (Arran Chiefs *or* other waxy variety).	1 teaspoonful apiece of: Chopped Tarragon.
1 teacupful Fresh Green Peas.	Chopped Chervil.
1 teacupful Diced Beetroot.	Chopped Parsley.
Salt and Pepper.	Chopped Shallot.
Salad Dressing.	

Cook, drain, and dry the vegetables, and dice the potatoes and beetroot. While still warm, place them in a salad bowl,

48

season, and add the finely chopped herbs. Pour over sufficient salad dressing to moisten thoroughly. (Olive oil and wine vinegar in the proportion of three-one may be used, or a mayonnaise or other salad dressing.) Toss and mix without breaking the potatoes. The salad may be decorated with a border of green peas and small triangles of beetroot, with a little chopped parsley sprinkled in the centre.

TOMATO AND SYBO SALAD

Tomatoes.
Syboes (Spring Onions).
Simple French Dressing.
Salt.
Pepper.

Put the tomatoes into boiling water for half a minute, then into cold, and remove the skin. Cut into slices, season with salt and pepper, and lay the slices, overlapping, in a long, narrow dish. Sprinkle generously with finely chopped syboes, and pour a little French dressing over all.

This is excellent with brown bread and butter and cheese, or, together with a potato salad, as an accompaniment to a cold-meat roll, cold chicken, etc., at a summer lunch.

HERRING SALAD

I teacupful Herring (Pickled or Salted).	I teacupful Beetroot.
I teacupful White Meat (Chicken, Veal, *or* Rabbit).	I teacupful Potato.
	I raw Apple.
	½ Pickled Gherkin.
	I dessertspoonful Sugar.
Salt and Pepper.	Plain French Dressing.

All the ingredients should be diced before measuring. The meat and vegetables are, of course, cooked. Turn all the ingredients into a bowl, and mix thoroughly. Moisten with French dressing. Heap on a bed of lettuce leaves, and decorate with chopped beetroot.

Pickled or marinated herring are used for this salad in Scotland. On the Continent, they use uncooked salted herring. These should be steeped overnight, preferably in milk.

D

ACCOMPANIMENTS and STUFFINGS

BUTTERED BARLEY

1 teacupful Barley.	1 dessertspoonful Butter.
3 teacupfuls Water.	Salt.

Put the barley into a saucepan with the cold water, bring to the boil, and add salt. Cook until the water has evaporated, stirring occasionally. Add the butter, and simmer very gently till tender.

Serve with mince, mutton, or other stew, or with a boiled fowl.

GREEN DUMPLINGS

8 oz. Flour.	Salt.
4 oz. Suet.	Pepper.
1 teaspoonful Baking Powder.	Cold Water.
	Young Green Shoots.

These dumplings are made only in spring, when things are covered with their first budding greenness. The dumplings are made in the ordinary way—chop the suet, add the dry ingredients, and mix to an elastic dough with cold water— but are made green with something of everything that grows in spring freshness which you gather unobtrusively during the day. Pick the green buds of hawthorn, the succulent tips of nettles, grass, and other green things—remember that in this condition nothing is poisonous. Include dandelion leaves, daisy stems, shoots of young corn, and turnip tops, or anything that tastes sweet and harmless. Wash and chop finely, and work into the dough until it is green through and through. Form into balls—small ones (one inch across) for soups, and larger for stews and meats. They go with almost anything, and play the part of a salad in wholesomeness.

CAR-CAKES

4 oz. Oatmeal.	1 Pinch of Cream of Tartar.
A pinch of Bicarbonate of Soda.	A dusting of Pepper.
A pinch of Salt.	Milk to mix.

Mix the dry ingredients in a bowl and stir in sufficient milk to make a thickish pouring batter. Fry in spoonfuls in hot bacon fat. If there is not enough fat to cover, turn when browned underneath. They take only a few minutes. Serve with the breakfast rashers.

HODGILS
(BORDER BROTH BALLS)

Oatmeal.	**Salt and Pepper.**
Chives.	**Beef Bree.**

When boiling beef for broth, the farmer's wife in the Borders frequently pops in some little oatmeal dumplings called hodgils.

Put a handful or two of oatmeal into a bowl, season with salt and pepper, add a few chopped chives, and moisten with the fatty stock skimmed from the top of the broth. Drop into the pot and boil for twenty minutes. Serve with the meat.

SKIRLIE
(SKIRL-IN-THE-PAN)

4 oz. Medium Oatmeal.	**2 oz. Suet** *or* **Dripping.**
1 *or* **2 Onions.**	**Salt and Pepper.**

Chop the suet finely. Put it into a very hot frying-pan, and when it is melted, add the finely chopped onion, and brown well. Now add enough oatmeal to absorb the fat—about four ounces—keeping the mixture fairly thick. Stir well for seven-ten minutes, till thoroughly cooked.

Skirlie may be served as an accompaniment to minced steak, roast grouse, etc. In cottage homes it is often served as a main dish, with a border of creamed potatoes.

OATMEAL DUMPLING

8 oz. Oatmeal.	**1 medium Onion.**
8 oz. Beef Suet.	**Salt.**
Black Pepper.	

Toast the oatmeal lightly in the oven. Chop the suet and onion. Mix them all, and season with salt and black pepper. Add no moisture, but tie up tightly, dry, in a cloth, leaving room to swell. Drop into a goblet of fast-boiling water, and boil slowly, uncovered, for $1\frac{1}{2}$ hours, keeping the dumpling under water all the time.

This is most commonly served with a boiled fowl, but is almost a meal in itself, and may be eaten with mashed potatoes.

A simpler dumpling can be made with half the quantity of suet, but it must then be bound with beaten egg or milk.

STAP
(SHETLAND)

2 Haddock Heads.	**Salt.**
2 Haddock Livers.	**Pepper.**

The fish must be perfectly fresh. Wash the livers, put them into a small jar (a jam jar will do), cover with paper, and set in a pan of boiling water. Let it cook for an hour. Clean, wash, and gently boil the haddock heads ; or boil the whole fish and then cut off the heads. Remove all the flesh from these, and add to the livers. Mix thoroughly, season, and dish neatly. Serve, piping hot, as an accompaniment to the fish.

KRAPPIN
(FISH LIVER STUFFING)

I lb. Fish Liver	**¼ lb. Fine Oatmeal** *or*
(*or* **2 teacupfuls**).	**¼ lb. Flour and ¼ lb.**
I teaspoonful Salt.	**Beremeal.**
	Sprinkling of Pepper.

If oatmeal is used, toast it lightly. Put all the ingredients into a bowl. Break down the liver with the hand, and work into the meal and seasoning until the mixture forms a firm ball. Use this to stuff either the muggie (stomach) or head of the fish. If ling liver is used, add a little more meal or the mixture may become too soft. The liver must, of course, be absolutely fresh.

Another way to cook the krappin is to put it into a paper bag, put this inside another paper bag, tie with string, plunge into boiling water, and boil for ten minutes. Serve as an accompaniment to the fish.

ROE KRAPPIN

Roe of Haddock *or* **Cod.**	**Parsley.**
Pounded Rusks *or* **Breadcrumbs.**	**Salt and Pepper.**
Butter.	**Egg.**

Parboil the roe, and mix it with double its bulk in pounded rusks or breadcrumbs. Add a good piece of butter and a little minced parsley ; season and bind with a beaten egg.

This may be used to stuff either the head or the body of the fish.

SAUCES

BREAD SAUCE

I cup Coarse Stale Breadcrumbs.	½ oz. Butter.
A small Onion.	Salt and Pepper.
I or 2 Cloves.	½ pint Milk.
I Blade of Mace.	I tablespoonful Cream.

Stick the clove into the peeled onion and put into a double boiler with the milk. Bring slowly to the boil, then add the mace and the crumbs, and stand in a hot place to infuse (without boiling) for thirty minutes. Remove the onion, clove, and mace, add the butter and seasoning, and stir over the fire till the butter is melted. Make very hot, and stir in the cream last thing.

Serve with roast chicken, turkey, or game.

EGG SAUCE

I½ oz. Butter.	½ pint Milk.
I oz. Flour.	½ pint White or Fish
Salt and Pepper.	Stock.
I or 2 Grains Nutmeg.	3 Hard-boiled Eggs.

Make a white roux with the butter and flour, and stir in gradually the hot milk and stock—white stock for chicken, fish stock, of course, for fish—or use all milk. Pass through a sieve, and re-heat. Chop the yolks and whites separately, and add to the sauce.

If you are making a coating sauce, add an extra half-ounce of both butter and flour, and add only the chopped whites to the sauce ; then when the fish or fowl is coated, grate the yolks over it. A little minced parsley or chives or (for fish) fennel may be added.

For a richer sauce, add the eggs to a well-seasoned Bechamel sauce, and stir in a spoonful or two of cream.

HEATHER HONEY SAUCE

1 cupful Heather Honey.	1 teaspoonful Butter.
⅓ Orange or Lemon.	1 Egg.

½ pint Water.

Heat the water and blend the honey with it. Add the juice and grated rind of half an orange or lemon, the butter, and the well-beaten egg. Cook in a double saucepan or in a small bowl in a saucepan of hot water, stirring constantly, for ten-fifteen minutes.

ROSE-HIP SAUCE
(DEESIDE)

Rose-hips.	Sugar.
Lemon.	Water.

Wash the hips in lukewarm water. Top-and-tail them, and remove the seeds. Bring to the boil enough water to cover the hips. (On no account use an aluminium pan.) Put in the hips when the water is just below boiling point, and simmer for fifteen minutes or till tender. Rub through a fine hair sieve with the back of a wooden spoon. Add sugar and lemon juice to taste.

Serve with cornflour shapes, milk puddings, etc.

COCKLE SAUCE

Cockles.	White Sauce.	Mustard.

To prepare the cockles, put a very little water into the fish-kettle or saucepan, fill half way up with cockles, set over the fire, and shake them now and then as they heat. As soon as the shells have opened, remove the pan—every moment's delay tends to toughen the cockles—and pick them out of their shells with a fork. Chop small as many as you require for your sauce.

Make a white sauce with half ounce flour, half ounce butter, a gill of milk, and a gill of cockle water, and stir in a dessert-spoonful of made mustard. Add two tablespoonfuls of chopped cockles, and heat thoroughly, but do not re-cook.

Serve with boiled cod or other white fish.

The remaining cockles may be served cold with vinegar in *hors-d'œuvre* dishes or saucers.

PUDDINGS and PIES

GLISTER PUDDING

4 oz. Flour.	2 tablespoonfuls Marmalade.
4 oz. Sugar.	2 teaspoonfuls Lemon Juice.
4 oz. Butter.	1 level teaspoonful Bicarbonate
2 Eggs.	of Soda.

Sift the flour. Beat the eggs. Cream the butter and sugar, and beat in the eggs and flour alternately, a little at a time. Dissolve the soda in a little water, and add along with the marmalade and lemon juice. Mix all lightly, turn into a greased pudding bowl, cover with a greased paper, and steam for two hours.

Half a teaspoonful of ground ginger may be added to the ingredients.

CROFTER'S PLUM PUDDING
(ORKNEY)

1 lb. Flour.	1 teaspoonful Bicarbonate of
8 oz. Suet.	Soda.
8 oz. Raisins.	1 or 2 Eggs.
6 oz. Sugar.	Ale to mix.

Sift the flour. Clean and stone the raisins. Chop the suet. Mix these together with the sugar, and add the beaten egg, with sufficient ale to make a soft dough. Add the soda dissolved in a spoonful of ale. Have a pot of water boiling. Wring a " clout " or pudding-cloth out of this, flour it well, and turn the pudding into it. Tie securely, plunge into boiling water, and boil for 2½-3 hours. Or steam in a greased bowl, allowing at least an hour extra.

This pudding requires no spice, as the ale, which in Orkney is home-brewed, gives it a distinctive and agreeable flavour; but spice may be added if desired. Breadcrumbs may be substituted for half the flour : this makes for lightness.

MELROSE PUDDING

8 oz. Flour.	1 teaspoonful Baking-powder.
4 oz. Butter.	2 Eggs.
4 oz. Sugar.	A few Raisins or Glacé
2 oz. Ground Almonds.	Cherries.
About a gill of Milk.	

Sift the flour. Beat the eggs. Cream the butter and sugar and beat in the eggs and flour alternately, adding the baking powder with the last spoonful of flour. Add the almonds and enough milk to let the batter drop easily from the spoon. Decorate a greased mould with raisins or halved glacé cherries, turn the pudding batter into it, covering with greased paper, and steam for 1½ hours. Leave for a minute or two before turning out. Serve with creamy custard or a sweet sauce.

URNEY PUDDING

4 oz. Flour.	½ teaspoonful Bicarbonate of
4 oz. Butter.	Soda.
2 oz. Sugar.	2 tablespoonfuls Jam.
2 Eggs.	(Strawberry for preference).

Sift the flour. Beat the eggs. Cream the butter and sugar, and beat in the eggs and flour alternately. Add the jam and, lastly, the soda dissolved in a teaspoonful of milk. Mix thoroughly, turn into a greased pudding bowl (which should be little more than half full), cover with greased paper, and steam for 1½ hours.

Serve with arrowroot sauce or creamy custard.

DUNFILLAN BRAMBLE PUDDING

Dunfillan Paste.	*Filling.*
4 oz. Flour.	1 lb. Brambles.
2 oz. Butter.	4 oz. Sugar.
2 oz. Castor Sugar.	Tiny pinch Salt.
1 Egg.	Flavouring:
¼ teaspoonful Baking-	Lemon or
Powder.	Cinnamon or
A pinch of Salt.	Clove or
2 tablespoonfuls Milk.	None.
Lemon Rind.	Water.

Cook the berries till soft with just enough water to cover. Turn into a pie-dish, sprinkling each layer with sugar. Add the salt and flavouring if desired.

Beat the butter and sugar to a cream. Beat the egg and add; then the sifted flour (with salt) and milk alternately. Add the baking-powder mixed with the last spoonful of flour, and flavour to taste with grated lemon rind. Spread smoothly over the fruit, and bake in a moderate oven for twenty minutes.

Other berries may be substituted for the brambles. The same batter may be poured over a thick layer of jam on a small ashet or a pie plate.

EVE'S PUDDING
(APPLES WITH DUNFILLAN PASTE)

Make as above, substituting stewed apples (sweetened and flavoured) for the brambles.

BARLEY PUDDING
(LOTHIANS)

8 oz. Barley.	**A pinch of Salt.**
4 oz. Currants.	**I quart Water.**

Put the barley into a pan with the cold water, bring slowly to the boil, and boil for 1½ hours. Add the currants (washed) and simmer for half an hour longer. Serve with sugar and thin cream or milk.

RHUBARB FLAN
WITH OATMEAL PASTRY

Pastry.	*Filling.*
1½ oz. Fine Oatmeal.	**I lb. Rhubarb.**
2½ oz. Flour.	**3-4 oz. Sugar.**
I oz. Margarine.	**I teaspoonful Cornflour.**
I oz. Lard.	**Water.**
I level teaspoonful Sugar.	**Carmine.**
Water.	

Wash and wipe the rhubarb and cut into one-inch pieces. Place in a jam jar with the sugar and two tablespoonfuls water and steam for forty-five minutes or till tender. Rub the fat into the flour and mix in the other dry ingredients. Add just enough cold water to make a stiff dough, and roll out to ¼-inch thick. Line a flan tin with the paste, trim edges, and prick all over. Bake in a moderate oven for thirty-forty minutes. Drain the cooked rhubarb and fill the flan with it. Measure a gill of the juice (adding water if required), heat it in a small pan, and thicken with the cornflour broken in a little water. Colour with a drop of carmine, and when the sauce is clear, pour it over the rhubarb. Serve the flan hot or cold.

PRUNE FLORY

½ lb. Prunes.	1 tablespoonful Lemon Juice.
2 oz. Sugar.	1 tablespoonful Port Wine.
	Puff Pastry.

Wash the prunes, soak them for an hour in cold water, then cook them gently in the same water till tender. Remove the stones and quarter the prunes. Obtain the meat from the stones, and add to the fruit. Add the sugar, lemon juice, and port wine. (The latter may be omitted, and a sprinkling of cinnamon substituted.) Heat two tablespoonfuls of the juice in a small pan, thicken with half a teaspoonful of cornflour broken in a little water, and cook for a minute or two. Line a pie-plate with puff pastry, cover with prunes, pour the thickened juice over them, and cover with another layer of paste. Flute the edges, and cut a slit in the centre to allow the steam to escape. Brush the top, if desired, with milk or beaten egg.

SAUCER PANCAKES

2 oz. Flour.	2 Eggs.
1½ oz. Butter.	½ pint Milk.
1 teaspoonful Castor Sugar.	Jam (Apricot for preference).

Sift the flour. Beat the eggs. Cream the butter and sugar, add the eggs, then the flour and milk alternately. Mix lightly, and pour into six buttered saucers. Bake in a hot oven for twenty minutes. Heat some jam. Turn out the pancakes, place some jam on half of each, and double up. Serve immediately.

COLD SWEETS

SCOTS TRIFLE

6 Sponge Cakes (Stale).	1 teaspoonful Vanilla Essence.
2 oz. Small Macaroons.	1 gill Fruit Syrup.
2 oz. Ratafia Biscuits.	4 Egg Yolks.
A few Pistachio Nuts.	2 Egg Whites.
Strawberry or Raspberry Jam.	1 pint Milk.
1 oz. Sugar.	½ pint Double Cream.

3-4 tablespoonfuls Sherry.

Put the milk and sugar into a saucepan and heat to boiling-point. Meanwhile, beat the eggs; then pour the hot milk over them, stirring well. Return to the pan, and stir over the fire till it thickens, but don't let it boil. Pour into a bowl, leave to cool a little, then add the vanilla. Split the sponge cakes, and spread thickly with jam. Cut up roughly, and arrange in a deep glass dish, placing the macaroons and ratafias between each layer. Pour the syrup and sherry over; then the custard. Leave to cool and soak. Whip the cream stiffly, sweeten and flavour with vanilla, and cover the trifle. Ornament with ratafias and chopped pistachio nuts. At Christmas-time, substitute green and red crystallised fruits.

ELDERBERRY SWEET
(LOTHIANS)

Elderberries.	**Sugar.**
Apples.	**Cornflour.**

Gather the berries that grow in shining black bunches on the wild elder bushes, and not the red-berried garden kind. Put them into a large jar (having removed all the stalks) and place in a slow oven or in a large pan of boiling water to extract the juice. Crush with a wooden spoon, strain through muslin, and squeeze out all the juice. To each pint of juice add ½ lb. sugar and half a dozen cloves (if liked). Bring to the boil, and simmer very gently for five minutes. Thicken with cornflour, allowing a scant two ounces to a pint of juice. Strain into a glass dish or individual glasses, and when it has set, cover with stewed and sieved apples. (These flavours combine well.) Top with whipped cream.

Do not mix milk with the elderberry juice: the colour changes to an alarming indigo.

STRAWBERRY SWEET
(ABERDEENSHIRE)

Ripe Strawberries.   **Castor Sugar.**
Red Currants.   **Cream.**

Take equal quantities of strawberries and sugar. Lay the berries flat on a large ashet, and over them sprinkle half the sugar. Shake the dish gently so that the berries may be sprinkled all over. Leave overnight. Next day strain the juice from some fresh red currants, and make a syrup by boiling this with the remainder of the sugar, allowing a pint of juice to $\frac{3}{4}$ lb. sugar. Simmer the strawberries in this until they are sufficiently jellied. Pour into individual glasses, and serve cold with double cream, plain or whipped.

CARAGEEN MOULD
(HEBRIDES)

$\frac{1}{2}$ **oz. Dried Carageen.**   **I Egg (optional).**
I$\frac{1}{2}$ pints Milk.   **Sugar to taste.**
Flavouring.

Carageen may be bought in packets, but in the Hebrides it is gathered in the rock-pools, washed free of salt and sand, spread out on the rocks or on a white cloth on the grass, and left for several days to bleach and dry. It is then put into muslin bags and hung up in a dry place, or stored in jars.

Wash the carageen and steep in cold water for at least twenty minutes. Put the required quantity of milk and seaweed into a saucepan, bring slowly to the boil, stir well until it thickens. Strain, add a well-beaten egg if desired, but of course do not re-boil. Add sugar to taste, and if you do not like the sea-flavour of the carageen, flavour with orange or lemon juice or sherry. Alternatively, you may simmer a bay leaf or a pinch of dried elder flowers, or a bit of lemon peel and another of cinnamon stick. In the islands it is usually eaten without additional flavouring, but the egg is popular.

Carageen contains iodine and sulphur, and is often recommended for chest troubles.

CRANACHAN or CREAM-CROWDIE

Double Cream.   **Castor Sugar.**
Coarse Oatmeal.   **Rum or Vanilla.**

Toast some oatmeal lightly before the fire, or in the oven, or in a thick-bottomed frying-pan over a gentle heat. This gives it an agreeable, somewhat nutty flavour. Beat a bowlful of cream to a stiff froth, and stir in a handful or two of oatmeal, making it not too substantial, *i.e.*, the cream must predominate. Sweeten to taste, and flavour with rum or essence of vanilla.

Throw in a few handfuls of fresh ripe berries—blaeberries raspberries, brambles, or others—and you have an excellent sweet.

SNACKS
SAVOURIES and MISCELLANEOUS

ANGLER'S OMELETTE

Fresh Herring Milts.   **Parsley.**
Smoked Salmon.   **Chervil.**
Salt.   **Chives.**
Cayenne.   **Butter.**
An Omelette *aux Fine Herbes*.

Take some fresh herring milts; sprinkle with salt, cayenne, and a little finely chopped parsley, chervil and chives. Wrap each milt in a thin slice of smoked salmon, and poach gently in butter. Make your omelette and set the salmon rolls in the centre. Roll up and serve immediately.

The omelette is made in the ordinary way with the addition of a teaspoonful of chopped fresh herbs—say parsley, chives, tarragon and chervil or watercress.

SCOTS EGGS

5 Eggs.	Breadcrumbs.
1 lb. Pork Sausage Meat.	Dripping.

Boil four of the eggs hard, as for salad. Beat up the fifth. Peel the boiled eggs, dip into the beaten egg and cover with well-seasoned sausage meat. Egg-and-breadcrumb them and fry in deep fat for ten minutes. Serve hot with good gravy or cold with salad.

Instead of sausage meat, the eggs may be coated with force-meat made of equal quantities of grated ham and breadcrumbs seasoned with a little chopped anchovy, a pinch of mixed spice, and salt and pepper to taste, bound with beaten egg. A well-seasoned rissole mixture may also be used.

COTTAGE CHEESE EGGS

A few scraps of Cheese.	A few drops Worcester Sauce.
A Pat of Butter.	A tablespoonful of Beer
A shake of Pepper (preferably Red).	(optional).
Salt to taste.	Some Fresh Eggs.
	Hot Buttered Toast.

Slice the cheese thinly, but do not grate it. Put it into a saucepan with very little butter and enough water to moisten. When it melts, add a shake of red pepper and a little Worcester Sauce. Let the cheese cook gently, adding, if you like, a table-spoonful of beer. When it is quite soft and liquid, break in a fresh egg for each person and stir vigorously over a gentle heat until the eggs are thoroughly incorporated and cooked, like buttered eggs. Pile on hot buttered toast.

FINDON TOASTS

2 oz. Finnan-Haddie (Cooked and Chopped).	Salt and Pepper.
½ oz. Butter.	Coralline Pepper.
1 tablespoonful Cream.	Cayenne.
1 Gherkin.	1 dessertspoonful Chopped Parsley.
6 Rounds Fried Bread.	

Melt the butter, put in the fish and the chopped gherkin, add the cream, salt (if required), pepper, and a few grains of cayenne. Pile on the rounds of bread, fork up neatly, and decorate with chopped parsley and coralline pepper. Serve very hot.

SCOTCH WOODCOCK

2 Egg Yolks.
1 oz. Butter.
Salt and Pepper.

3-4 tablespoonfuls Cream.
1 teaspoonful Chopped Parsley.
Anchovy Butter.

2 Slices of Hot Toast.

ANCHOVY BUTTER

4-5 Preserved Anchovies.
2 oz. Butter.

Salt.
Pepper.

Prepare the anchovy butter by washing the anchovies in warm water, pounding them in a mortar with the butter, and passing the mixture through a sieve. Keep in a cool place till required. Anchovy essence may be substituted for the whole anchovies, but is not so satisfactory.

Halve and trim the slices of toast and spread with the prepared butter. Pour over a hot sauce made as follows :

Put egg yolks, butter, cream, and parsley into a bowl, add seasoning, stand the bowl over a pan of hot water and stir over the fire until the sauce thickens.

Serve very hot.

KIPPER TOASTS

Kipper.
Cayenne.

Mustard.
Buttered Toast.

Grill a kipper, strip the flesh from the skin and bones, and pound well. Season with cayenne. Spread the buttered toast very thinly with made mustard, and then with the kipper cream.

BUCHAN BEANS

8 oz. Haricot Beans.
4 oz. Fat Bacon.

A few Chives.
Pepper.

Steep the beans overnight, boil, and drain thoroughly. Dice the bacon and fry slowly until the fat is melted. Tumble the beans into the frying-pan, mixing them well with the bacon fat. Season. When thoroughly hot, turn into a heated vegetable dish and sprinkle with chopped chives.

PORRIDGE
(THE AGE-OLD METHOD)

Oatmeal, like coffee, must be kept closely packed and air-tight. Quality, too, is important. Far too much oatmeal on the market is mass-milled by a process that injures both its flavour and its nutritive qualities, and far too many cooks not bred in the tradition steep it for hours on end and cook it for hours on end, and eventually serve up a gluey, flavourless mess with sugar, and, to crown all, *hot* milk ! But who that has tasted porridge properly made and served with cream or rich milk, will deny that it is food for the gods ?

Home-milled Meal.   **Salt.**   **Fresh Spring Water.**

Allow for each person a breakfastcupful of water, a handful of oatmeal (about 1¼ oz.) of medium quality, and a small salt-spoonful of salt. Put the water on in the porridge pot (it is advisable to keep a thick-bottomed pot exclusively for porridge), and as soon as the water reaches boiling-point add the oatmeal, letting it fall in a steady rain from the left hand whilst you stir it with the right, using either a spurtle or the *handle* of a long wooden spoon. When the porridge is boiling steadily, draw it to the side, cover and cook gently. Cook for ten minutes or so before adding salt. (If added before or along with the meal, it has a tendency to harden the grain.) Boil for twenty-thirty minutes in all, according to taste and the quality of the grain. (Some old farmers will not allow it to be boiled longer than ten minutes.) Ladle into wooden bowls or *cold* soup plates, and serve with small individual bowls of cream or rich milk. Sup preferably with a horn spoon (porridge is apt to over-heat a metal spoon), and dip each spoonful of porridge into the cold milk before conveying it to the mouth.

Perfect porridge requires a fourth ingredient—hill or sea air !

BROSE

Brose was formerly the universal ploughman's breakfast in Scotland—but was popular, too, in all ranks of society—and did much to build up brain and brawn.

Oatmeal.   **Butter (optional).**
Salt.   **Water.**

Put a " gowpen " of home-milled meal (as much as you can lift between your palms) into a " timmer caup " (wooden bowl) or porringer, with a little salt, and pour over it enough boiling water to wet it thoroughly. Stir it up (the ploughmen used to use the shank of a horn spoon) and allow it to stand for a few minutes by the fireside to let the meal swell. Sup with a mug of new milk.

A knob of butter is often stirred into the brose. On special occasions fat brose is served, when, instead of water, the fatty top of the beef bree is stirred into the meal. This used to be commonly served as Yule Brose on Yule morning.

BLACK PUDDINGS

1 quart Fresh Pig's Blood.	Onions.
½ pint Milk.	1 oz. Oatmeal.
1 lb. Shredded Suet.	Salt and Pepper.

Let the blood run into a deep dish, stirring all the time. Add a teaspoonful of salt, stir again, and rub through a hair sieve. Add the milk, and mix well. Put in the suet, the minced onions, the oatmeal (previously lightly toasted in the oven), and the salt and pepper. Mix well, fill the skins not quite full, and tie them in equal lengths. Have ready a potful of boiling water. Throw a little cold water in to put it off the boil just before you put in the puddings (to keep them from bursting). After five minutes prick them over with a large needle, then let them cook gently for about two hours.

Hang them up in a dry, cool place till required. Heat through in hot water and broil, or slice and fry in dripping.

WHITE OR MEALIE PUDDINGS

2 lbs. Oatmeal.	Salt.
1 lb. Beef Suet.	Jamaica Pepper.
2 Onions.	Sugar (optional).
Tripe Skins.	

Toast the oatmeal lightly in the oven or before the fire. Mince finely the fresh beef suet and the onions, and add to the oatmeal along with the salt, pepper, and one-two teaspoonfuls of sugar. Mix thoroughly and fill the prepared tripe-skins, leaving room for swelling. Tie the ends, and drop into boiling water. Prick occasionally with a fork to prevent bursting. Cook for an hour.

The puddings will keep for months if hung up and kept

E

dry, or, better, if kept buried in oatmeal in the girnel or meal chest. When required, warm through in hot water, dry, and brown in hot dripping.

GRUEL

1¼ oz. Oatmeal.	1 teaspoonful Honey
A pinch of Salt.	or Syrup.
½ pint Water.	A pat of Butter.

Soak the oatmeal in the water (cold) for half an hour or longer, then turn into a sieve placed over a saucepan and press the liquid through (using a wooden spoon). This contains all the flour of the meal, which should be left as dry as possible. A little cold water may be added to help extract the flour. Place the pan over heat and stir till it boils. Add salt and cook gently for ten-fifteen minutes, stirring all the time. Withdraw, and stir in the butter and honey or syrup.

This is an old-fashioned cure for a cold or sore throat, and is usually highly popular with the invalid.

SOWANS

In the days of local mills, when the oats that had been winnowed and threshed were returned as meal, the miller always sent with it a bag of " sids "—the inner husks of the oat grain—to which adheres some of the finest and most nutritive substance of the meal. This was made into a kind of smooth pudding or gruel called *sowans* (Gael. *sughan*, pronounced soo-an)—an ancient dish of Celtic origin. It has a slightly sour taste, but usually " grows on " one ; and it is said to be an ideal diet for invalids, especially for dyspeptics.

Oatmeal Sids.　　　　**Salt.**　　　　**Water.**

Put a quantity of sids into the sowan-bowie (a narrow-mouthed wooden tub resembling a small barrel with an open end) or an earthenware jar, and pour over them twice their bulk of lukewarm water. The sids rise to the surface and must be pressed down with a spatula or wooden spoon till all are wet. Leave them in a warm place until they are quite sour. They will take anything from four to five days in hot weather to a fortnight in very cold weather. A week is a fair average. Then comes the process known as " the syein' o' the so'ons," when the contents of the bowie are poured over a fine sieve (sye) into a wide-mouthed vessel, the sids being squeezed between the hands to get all the goodness out of them   A little cold water should be added to wash out any remaining sediment. The sids are now thrown away, and the liquid is allowed to stand for two days longer, until all the starchy matter has sunk to the bottom. (This contains practically all the nutritious properties of the oatmeal in its most easily digested form.)

When required for use, pour off the clear liquid and put some of the sediment into a saucepan, allowing a gill for each person, with two gills of water and salt to taste. Bring to the boil, stirring continuously, and cook gently for ten-twenty minutes, or until thick and creamy. Serve like porridge in small wooden bowls or deep plates, with new milk or cream.

HATTIT KIT
(A VERY OLD HIGHLAND DISH)

2 pints Buttermilk.   **Sugar.**
2 pints New Milk.   **Nutmeg.**
          Double Cream.

Warm the buttermilk slightly before milking-time. Carry the vessel to the side of a cow and milk into it a pint of milk. Stir well together. At the next milking, add another pint and stir again. Let it stand till it firms and gathers a " hat." Remove the curd, place it on a hair sieve, and press the whey through until the curd is stiff. Put into a mould and leave for half an hour. Turn out and strew with sugar and nutmeg (or cinnamon if preferred), and serve with thick cream.

CROWDIE
(HIGHLANDS)

3 pints New Milk.   **I teaspoonful Rennet.**
Salt to taste.   **I tablespoonful Double Cream.**

Add the rennet to the milk while still warm from the cow, or, alternatively, warmed to blood heat. When the curd forms, cut it up and leave in a warm place to separate it better from the whey, but do not overheat, or it will toughen. When the whey rises to the top, turn the whole dish into a colander and leave to drain. Put the curd into a bowl, add a tablespoonful of double cream and salt to taste, and mix until soft and creamy. Form into a round like a cream cheese, and serve with oatcakes and butter.

FARM CHEESE PATTIES

4 oz. Grated Cheese.	**Salt and Pepper.**
A pinch of Nutmeg.	**2 Eggs.**
A pinch of Cayenne.	**2 cupfuls Milk.**

Short Pastry.

Line some patty-pans with thin short pastry. Beat the eggs lightly, stir in the cheese and seasonings, and lastly add the milk. Mix well, then fill the lined patty-pans. Cover each with a thin layer of pastry and pinch the edges together. Bake in a hot over for ten minutes, then reduce the heat and bake till the pastry is nicely browned.

HERRING ROES ON OATCAKES

6 Milt Roes.	**½ teaspoon Salt.**
1-2 Bay Leaves.	**1 gill Vinegar.**
6 White Peppercorns.	**½ pint Water.**
2 teaspoons Chopped Parsley.	**Sprinkling of Lemon Juice.**

6 Small Oatcakes *or* **Rounds of Toast.**

Wipe the roes carefully in a soft cloth and place in a deep dish. Put into a small saucepan the water, vinegar, salt, peppercorns and bay leaves, bring to boiling-point and strain over the roes. Cover with a greased paper and bake for ten minutes in a moderate oven.

Butter the oatcakes, coil a drained roe on each, dot with tiny bits of butter or margarine and place under a hot grill for two or three minutes. Sprinkle with lemon juice and parsley and serve very hot.

PRUNE SAVOURIES

Prunes.	**Red Pepper.**
Finnan-haddie.	**Thick Cream.**

Soak some large French prunes, extract the stones and fill the cavities with a stuffing of cooked finnan-haddie flavoured with red pepper and beaten with thick cream to a smooth *mousse*. Serve hot on squares of fried bread.

SCONES AND TEABREAD

BUTTERMILK BREAD

1 lb. Flour.	1 teaspoonful Bicarbonate of Soda.
1 oz. Sugar.	1 teaspoonful Cream of Tartar.
1 oz. Butter.	A pinch of Salt.

Buttermilk or Thick Sour Milk.

Sift the flour into a basin. Add the soda, cream of tartar, salt and sugar. Rub in the butter. (If good farm-house buttermilk is used, the butter may be omitted.) Make into a soft dough with the milk. About half a pint should be enough. Put into a floured loaf-tin and bake in a moderate oven for forty-five minutes or till risen and firm.

BAPS

(SCOTS BREAKFAST ROLLS)

1 lb. Flour.	1 teaspoonful Sugar.
2 oz. Lard.	1 small teaspoonful Salt.
1 oz. Yeast.	½ pint Milk-and-Water.

Sift the flour into a warm bowl and mix in the salt. Rub the lard in thoroughly with the finger-tips. In another bowl cream the yeast and sugar (that is, work them together with a wooden spoon till liquid) ; make the milk and water tepid and add to the yeast ; then strain into the flour. Make into a soft dough, cover, and set to rise for an hour in a warm place. Knead lightly, divide into pieces of equal size, and form into oval shapes about three inches long and two wide. Brush with milk or water (to give a glaze), and if " floury baps " are desired, dust them with flour just after brushing them, and again just before they go into the oven. Place the baps on a greased and floured tin and set again in a warm place for fifteen minutes, to prove. To prevent blisters, press a finger into the centre of each before they are placed in the oven. Bake in a hot oven for fifteen or twenty minutes.

Baps appear exclusively on the breakfast table, and should be eaten warm (or re-warmed) from the oven.

WHITE BANNOCKS or SODA SCONES

1 lb. Flour.	½ teaspoonful Tartaric Acid.
¾ teaspoonful Bicarbonate of Soda.	Buttermilk or Thick Sour Milk to mix.
½ teaspoonful Salt.	

Sift the dry ingredients in a baking-bowl and mix to a very soft dough with the milk. Roll out or pat out on a floured board to a half-inch thickness. Cut into two rounds or bannocks, using a plate. They may be baked whole (farm-house style) or cut across into six or eight scones. Cook on a fairly hot floured girdle (put this on to heat before you begin) for ten minutes, turning at half time and finishing at a rather lower heat.

BARLEY BANNOCKS

Make exactly as above, but use barley meal and white flour in the proportion of three to one ; or, if you prefer, use equal quantities. An all-barley bannock tastes too sour to please the unaccustomed palate.

WHOLEMEAL SCONES

6 oz. Wholemeal.	½ teaspoonful Salt.
6 oz. Flour.	3 oz. Butter
2 teaspoonfuls Baking Powder.	1 dessertspoonful Syrup.
	Milk to mix.

Mix the wholemeal, flour, salt, and baking-powder. Stir in the syrup (slightly melted) and sufficient milk to make a soft dough. Roll out lightly, making it rather thin. Cut into scones with a round cutter, 1½ inches in diameter. Place on a floured baking-sheet and bake in a moderate oven for ten-fifteen minutes.

RICH CREAM SCONES

½ lb. Flour.	1 oz. Butter.
1 teaspoonful Baking Powder.	1 Egg.
A small pinch of Salt.	1 gill Sour Cream.

Sift the flour and baking-powder into a basin; add the salt, and rub in the butter lightly with the finger-tips. Make a hollow in the centre, and into it pour the cream and the well-beaten egg. Make into a soft dough and turn on to a floured board. Roll out lightly, or pat out to a half-inch in thickness, prick all over with a fork, cut into rounds, and fire on the girdle or in the oven. When cooked, split open and spread with butter and/or jam.

A teaspoonful or more of castor sugar may be added if desired.

WHITE OVEN SCONES

1 lb. Flour.	½ teaspoonful Salt.
1 teaspoonful Bicarbonate of Soda.	1 oz. Sugar.
2 teaspoonfuls Cream of Tartar.	3 oz. Butter.
Milk to mix.	1 Egg.

Sift the flour, soda and cream of tartar into a baking-bowl; add the salt and sugar; rub in the butter. Beat the egg and pour into a well in the flour mixture, with enough milk to make a very soft dough. Turn on to a floured board, sprinkle with flour, roll out or pat out to a half-inch thickness, cut into rounds or triangles, and bake in a pretty quick oven for ten-fifteen minutes.

If you use buttermilk (which makes a better scone), halve the quantity of cream of tartar.

Serve warm (not hot) for tea, and spread with butter and/or jam.

TREACLE (MOLASSES) SCONES

½ lb. Flour.	½ teaspoonful Cinnamon.
¼ teaspoonful Bicarbonate of Soda.	½ teaspoonful Ginger.
¼ teaspoonful Cream of Tartar (scant).	1 teaspoonful Sugar.
	1 tablespoonful Treacle.
¼ teaspoonful Salt.	1½ oz. Butter.
	Buttermilk to mix.

Rub the butter into the flour; add all the other dry ingredients and mix well. Melt the treacle and mix with a little buttermilk. Stir into the flour mixture, adding just enough milk to make a stiff dough. Knead lightly, roll out to three-quarter inch thick, form into a round, and cut into eight triangular pieces. Place on a greased tin and bake in a good oven for ten-fifteen minutes.

ABERDEEN DATE SCONE

8 oz. Flour.	1 oz. Butter.
½ teaspoonful Bicarbonate of Soda.	2 oz. Chopped Dates.
1 teaspoonful Cream of Tartar.	1 dessertspoonful Syrup.
	1 Egg.
1 cupful Milk.	

Grease and flour a sandwich tin. Sieve the flour, soda, and cream of tartar. Rub in the butter. Add the finely chopped dates. Beat the egg. Melt the syrup and add to the dry ingredients along with the milk and half the beaten egg. The dough should be moderately soft. Flour the surface and turn into the prepared tin, flattening the dough lightly to fit it. Brush over with the remainder of the egg, and bake in a good oven for about twenty minutes.

When cool, split and butter, and cut across into six or eight pieces.

POTATO SCONES

½ lb. Boiled Potatoes.	½ oz. Butter or Margarine.
2 oz. Flour.	A pinch of Salt.

In cottage homes, these scones are usually made just after the midday meal, when the left-over potatoes are still warm.

Heat your girdle. Mash the potatoes smoothly, adding dots of butter and salt if required, and beat well. Gradually work in as much flour as the potatoes will absorb. Turn on to a floured board and roll out till very thin. Cut into bannocks (using a meat plate) and then into farls. Prick all over with a fork and bake on a fairly hot girdle for about five minutes, turning them once.

Cool in a towel; or, if preferred, butter them at once, roll up, and serve hot. They should be eaten the day they are made, and are good with butter and honey, syrup, or jam.

DROP SCONES

8 oz. Flour.	1 tablespoonful Castor Sugar.
½ teaspoonful Bicarbonate of Soda.	1 Egg.
½ Teaspoonful Cream of Tartar.	Buttermilk to mix.

Sieve the dry ingredients into a bowl. Make a well in the centre, break the egg into it, and add a little buttermilk. Beat till smooth with a wooden spoon, then beat in gradually enough buttermilk to make a thick, creamy batter—a scant half-pint in all. Have ready a moderately hot girdle, grease it slightly— just enough to prevent sticking—with a piece of suet wrapped in a white rag, and drop on the batter, a spoonful at a time, until the girdle is full. The scones should be a neat round shape. (If you cannot trust your hand and eye, place a greased scone-cutter on the girdle and drop the batter through, removing the cutter in a minute or two). When the scones are covered with bubbles, slip a broad knife under them, and if they are of a golden-brown colour, turn them and brown the other side. Turn only once. Lay them on a clean towel and keep them wrapped in the towel till cool, unless they are to be eaten hot from the girdle.

These scones may be made with sweet (*i.e.* fresh) milk, when a double quantity of cream of tartar will be required ; but the quality is not quite the same. A morsel of butter may be rubbed into the flour to enrich the scones. Serve as fresh as possible with butter and/or jam.

Stale drop scones are very good fried up with the breakfast bacon.

TEA PANCAKES
(ORKNEY)

1 teacupful Flour.	1 Egg.
1 tablespoonful Sifted Sugar.	Milk to mix.
1 saltspoonful Salt.	Suet to grease girdle.

Beat the egg. Sift the flour into a bowl and add the sugar and salt. Add gradually, stirring all the time, enough milk to make a batter of the consistency of thin cream. Add the egg and beat well. Have ready a fairly hot girdle, rub it over with a piece of suet wrapped in a clean white rag, put on a large table-spoonful of the batter, spreading it out as thinly and making it as round as possible. It should brown very quickly; then turn and brown the other side.

The pancakes may be made in a small omelette pan greased with lard.

Turn on to a clean towel and cover. When cool, spread with butter and/or jam and roll up. They must be eaten fresh, and the closer to tea-time they are made the better.

OATCAKES
(TRADITIONAL METHOD)

4 oz. Oatmeal.
I teaspoonful Fat.
Hot Water.

A pinch of Salt.
A pinch of Bicarbonate of Soda.

As the dough stiffens when lying about, it is best to make a bannock at a time, using the above quantities, the next being prepared whilst the one is on the girdle.

Put the oatmeal into a bowl and add the salt and soda. Melt a teaspoonful of dripping or fat. (Bacon fat, goose fat, or poultry fat are all excellent.) Make a well in the centre of the meal, put in the dripping, and add as much hot water as will make a stiff paste. Rub plenty of oatmeal on to the baking board; turn out the mixture and form into a smooth ball. Knead and roll out as thinly as possible. Rub constantly on both sides with dry meal to prevent sticking, and keep the edges as even as possible by pinching with finger and thumb. Give a final rub with meal, cut into a round, using a plate, and then cut the bannock into farls (fardels or quarters) or into smaller pieces. Place on a moderately hot girdle and bake steadily till the cakes curl up at the edge; then toast the other side slightly before a clear fire or finish in the oven.

If you have neither a girdle nor a thick-bottomed frying-pan, you may bake the oatcakes in a moderate oven for twenty-thirty minutes, till quite dry and curled at the edges.

Buttered oatcakes are particularly good with marmalade, honey, cheese, fried herrings, and sardines.

CAKES AND SHORTBREADS

DUNDEE CAKE

10 oz. Flour.	2 oz. Whole Almonds.
8 oz. Butter.	3 oz. Ground Almonds.
8 oz. Sugar.	Rind of 1 Orange.
4 oz. Currants.	A pinch of Salt.
4 oz. Raisins.	$\frac{3}{4}$ teaspoonful Bicarbonate of
4 oz. Sultanas.	Soda.
4 oz. Candied Peel	1 teaspoonful Milk.
(Orange and Lemon).	5 Eggs.

Sift the flour. Prepare the fruit. Chop the peel. Blanch and split the whole almonds. Grate the orange rind. Beat the eggs. Cream the butter and sugar, and add the eggs and flour alternately, beating well. Add the fruit, ground almonds, grated rind, and salt, but omit the split almonds. Lastly, add the soda dissolved in the milk. Turn into a tin that has been greased and lined with greased paper, cover the surface with the split almonds, and bake in a rather slow oven for three hours.

SCOTS SEED CAKE

7 oz. Flour.	2 oz. Almonds.
4 oz. Butter.	$\frac{1}{4}$ teaspoonful Ground Cinnamon.
4 oz. Sugar.	$\frac{1}{4}$ teaspoonful Grated Nutmeg.
2 oz. Citron Peel.	1 teaspoonful Baking Powder.
1 oz. Orange Peel.	3 Eggs.
1 oz. Lemon Peel.	A few Caraway Comfits.

Sieve the flour and spices together. Blanch and chop the almonds. Cut the candied peel into thin shreds. Beat the eggs. Cream the butter and sugar, and beat in the flour and eggs alternately, mixing the baking-powder with the last spoonful of flour. Add the almonds and peel. The batter should drop easily from the spoon, so, if necessary, add a little milk. Turn into a cake-tin lined with greased paper, strew some caraway comfits over, and bake in a moderate oven for an hour longer, till well risen and firm.

SNOW CAKE

8 oz. Arrowroot.	3 Whites of Egg.
8 oz. Butter.	Lemon, Vanilla, or
4 oz. Castor Sugar.	Almond Essence.

Beat the butter to a cream. Mix the arrowroot with the sugar, and stir gradually into the butter, beating well. Whisk the egg whites to a stiff froth, add, and beat for twenty minutes. Add flavouring to taste. Pour into a buttered tin and bake in a moderate oven until well risen and firm—about an hour.

PORTREE PLUM CAKE

1 lb. Flour.	1 teaspoonful Bicarbonate of Soda.
1 lb. Currants.	
½ lb. Butter.	1 teaspoonful Cinnamon.
½ lb. Demerara Sugar.	1 teaspoonful Grated Nutmeg.
¼ lb. Candied Peel.	3 Eggs.
½ pint Brisk Stout.	

Rub the butter into the flour till it resembles breadcrumbs. Add all the dry ingredients. Beat the eggs, and add gradually with the stout. Mix thoroughly. Turn into a cake-tin lined with greased paper, and bake in a moderate oven for two-three hours. (Test with a skewer.).

This cake should be kept for at least a week before cutting, and improves with keeping.

STRAWBERRY SANDWICH
(ABERDEENSHIRE)

3 oz. Flour.	1 cupful Strawberries.
4 oz. Sugar.	1 gill Double Cream.
1 teaspoonful Baking Powder.	1 White of Egg.
1 tablespoonful Hot Water.	1½ oz. Castor Sugar.
3 Eggs.	½ teaspoonful Vanilla Essence.

Separate the yolks and whites of the eggs. Beat the whites stiffly. Add one yolk and beat three minutes; do the same with the second and the third; then add the sugar and water, and beat five minutes. Sift the flour and baking-powder, and stir in lightly. Turn into two prepared sandwich tins and bake for twenty minutes in a fairly hot oven. Turn out and cool on a wire tray.

Mash the strawberries with a fork. Beat the egg-white till stiff. Whisk the cream till quite thick, and fold in the egg-white. Add the sugar and strawberries by degrees, and flavour with vanilla. Spread one cake with the filling, and place the other on top.

GRANNY'S LOAF

12 oz. Flour.	I teaspoonful Ground Cloves.
8 oz. Sugar.	I teaspoonful Ground Caraways.
4 oz. Butter.	I teaspoonful Cinnamon.
8 oz. Sultanas.	I teaspoonful (small) Bicarbonate
I Egg.	of Soda.

A little Milk.

Rub the butter into the flour with the finger-tips until it is like breadcrumbs. Add the sugar, sultanas, and spices, and mix well. Beat the egg. Dissolve the soda in a little milk. Add both to the dry ingredients, but use only enough milk to *moisten* the cake. On no account make it wet. Turn the mixture into a buttered cake tin, and place in a hot oven, but lower the heat as soon as the cake has risen. Bake for about $1\frac{1}{2}$ hours.

A richer cake can be made by using two eggs and less or no milk.

BLACK BUN

I lb. Flour.	½ teaspoonful Black Pepper.
2 lbs. Currants.	Small teaspoonful Bicarbonate
2 lbs. Valencia Raisins.	of Soda.
½ lb. Almonds.	1-2 tablespoonfuls Brandy.
½ lb. Mixed Candied Peel.	Buttermilk or Egg to moisten.
4 oz. Sugar.	
½ oz. Ground Cloves or	
Cinnamon.	Crust:
½ oz. Ground Ginger.	I lb. Flour.
I teaspoonful Jamaica	½ lb. Butter.
Pepper.	Water.

Wash and dry the currants. Stone the raisins. Blanch and chop the almonds. Chop the peel. Sift the flour into a basin, and add the sugar, spices, and prepared fruits. If buttermilk is used, stir the soda into it before moistening the cake; if egg, add the soda with the dry ingredients. Add the brandy first so that the mixture should not become wet. It should be merely moist.

Make a paste by rubbing the butter into the flour and adding just enough water to make a stiff dough, and roll out thinly. Grease a large cake-tin and line it evenly with the paste, retaining enough to cover the top. Trim the edges, put the mixture in, flatten the surface, moisten the edges of the paste with cold water, put on the lid of pastry, and make all secure and neat. With a skewer make four holes right down to the bottom of the cake; then prick all over with a fork, brush with beaten egg, and bake in a moderate oven for about four hours.

This cake should be made several weeks, or even months, before it is to be used, so that it may mature and mellow. Many housewives, indeed, allow it a full twelvemonth.

Black Bun always appears on Hogmanay, or New Year's Eve.

DOUGLAS HONEY CAKE

4 oz. Flour.	1 teaspoonful Baking
4 oz. Castor Sugar.	Powder.
4 oz. Butter.	½ cupful Honey.
4 oz. Ground Almonds.	2 Eggs.

Sift the flour and baking-powder together, and add half the ground almonds. Cream the butter and sugar, and add gradually the well-beaten eggs and the flour, a little of each alternately. Beat thoroughly, and pour into two small well-greased sandwich tins. Bake in a hot oven for about twenty minutes, or until well risen and firm. Blend the remainder of the ground almonds with the honey, and when the cakes are cold, spread one with the mixture and place the other on top. If desired, it may be iced and decorated, but it is usually eaten plain.

EDINBURGH GINGERBREAD

8 oz. Flour.	1 level teaspoonful Bicarbonate
4 oz. Butter.	of Soda.
4 oz. Treacle.	1 level teaspoonful Cinnamon.
2 oz. Sugar.	1 level teaspoonful Cloves.
4 oz. Raisins.	1 heaped teaspoonful Ginger.
2 oz. Almonds.	2 Eggs.

Sift the flour, soda, and spices into a basin. Clean and stone the raisins, blanch and split the almonds, and add to the flour mixture.

Put the butter, sugar, and treacle into a small saucepan and bring to the boil. Beat the two eggs, and pour the boiling treacle over them, stirring vigorously. Pour this mixture on to the dry ingredients and beat thoroughly. Put into a buttered cake-tin and bake for an hour or longer in a very moderate oven.

INVERNESS GINGERBREAD

12 oz. Flour.	4 oz. Candied Lemon Peel.
4 oz. Fine Oatmeal.	1 oz. Green Ginger.
8 oz. Butter.	½ gill Cream *or* Rich Milk.
12 oz. Treacle.	1 teaspoonful Bicarbonate of Soda.

Mix the flour, soda and oatmeal together. Cream the butter, and beat in the flour mixture and cream alternately. Stir in the slightly melted treacle, then add the ginger and peel cut into fine shreds. Work the whole into a light dough, turn into a well-greased tin, and bake in a moderate oven for about forty-five minutes.

SELKIRK BANNOCK

2 lbs. Baker's Dough.	8 oz. Sugar.
4 oz. Butter *or* Margarine.	12 oz. Sultanas.
4 oz. Lard.	4 oz. Candied Orange Peel.

You may either make your own dough or procure it from the baker. Into it rub the butter and lard until melted, but not oiled. Then work in the sugar, sultanas, and finely chopped peel. Turn the dough into a buttered tin, let it stand in a warm place for thirty minutes to rise, and then bake in a good steady oven.

MONTROSE CAKES

4 oz. Flour.	1 dessertspoonful Brandy.
4 oz. Butter.	1 teaspoonful Rose Water.
4 oz. Castor Sugar.	3 Eggs, *or* 2 eggs and
3 oz. Currants.	1 tablespoonful Milk.
A pinch of Nutmeg.	½ teaspoonful Baking Powder.

Sift the flour; wash the currants; beat the eggs. Cream the butter and sugar, and beat in gradually the eggs, flour, and nutmeg. Add the baking-powder with the last spoonful of flour; but if three eggs are used it should be omitted. Add the brandy and rose-water. Beat thoroughly, and put into buttered patty-pans, half filling them. Bake for fifteen minutes in a hot oven.

PAISLEY ALMOND CAKES

2 oz. Cornflour.	**3 oz. Butter.**
2 oz. Rice Flour.	**3 oz. Castor Sugar.**
I small teaspoonful Baking Powder.	**1½ oz. Ground Almonds.**
	2 Eggs.

Grease a dozen patty-pans. Sieve the flours and baking-powder together. Beat the eggs. Cream the butter and sugar, and beat in the eggs and flour alternately. When white and creamy, stir in the ground almonds lightly. Half fill the tins, and bake in a moderate oven for ten-fifteen minutes. Turn out and cool on a wire tray.

MELTING MOMENTS

8 oz. Cornflour.	**I teaspoonful Baking Powder.**
6 oz. Butter.	**Grated Lemon Rind.**
3 oz. Castor Sugar.	**2 Eggs.**

Grease two dozen small patty-tins. Cream the butter and sugar, and add a flavouring of grated lemon rind. Beat the eggs and add them, alternately, with the cornflour, to the butter and sugar, mixing the baking-powder with the last spoonful of cornflour. Put a teaspoonful of the mixture into each patty-pan. Bake in a good oven for ten-twelve minutes.

These make delicious little afternoon tea-cakes.

SCOTS SHORTBREAD

8 oz. Finest Pastry Flour.	**8 oz. Best Butter.**
4 oz. Rice Flour.	**4 oz. Fine Castor Sugar.**

Only the finest materials should be used for shortbread. The flour should be dried and sieved, and the butter squeezed free of all moisture.

Put the butter and sugar on a board and work with the hand until thoroughly incorporated. Mix the two flours, and gradually work into the butter and sugar until the dough resembles short crust. Do not roll out, but press with the hand into two round cakes, either in oiled and floured wooden short-bread moulds, or on a sheet of baking-paper. The best thickness is ¾ inch for a cake eight inches in diameter. Pinch the edges neatly with finger and thumb, and prick all over with a fork.

Put into a fairly hot oven, but reduce the heat presently and allow the shortbread to crisp off to a pale golden brown.

Many Scottish housewives maintain that shortbread can be baked to perfection only in an oven heated with coal.

The Hogmanay shortbread is usually larger and thicker than the usual size, and is often decorated in the centre with candied citron peel and " sweetie almonds " (almond comfits). It is advisable to bind two or three thicknesses of paper round it in baking, so that the edges do not get scorched before the centre is fired.

PITCAITHLY BANNOCK

13 oz. Pastry Flour.	4 oz. Castor Sugar.
2 oz. Rice Flour.	2 oz. Sweet Almonds.
8 oz. Butter.	2 oz. Candied Orange Peel.

Blanch the almonds and mince them and the peel very finely. Work the butter and sugar together with the hand on a pastry board or slab ; work in the rice flour ; then the sifted pastry flour. Strew with the minced almonds and peel, press them in, and knead till quite smooth, but do not over-knead. Wrap in grease-proof paper and leave until next day.

Re-knead the paste, and finish as for Scots Shortbread.

PETTICOAT TAILS
(PETITES GATELLES)

12 oz. Flour.	1½ oz. Castor Sugar.
4 oz. Butter.	¼ oz. Caraway Seeds.
½ gill Milk.	

Mix the caraway seeds with the flour. Melt the butter in the milk. Make a well in the middle of the flour and pour in the milk and butter. Add the sugar. Mix thoroughly and knead a little—if too much, it will not be short. Roll out rather thin, and cut the cake by running a paste-cutter round a dinner plate inverted on the paste. Cut a cake from the centre of this one with a small saucer or a large tumbler. Keep this inner circle whole, and cut the outer one into eight *petticoat-tails*. Bake on greased paper laid on a tin, in a moderate oven. Remove when brown and crisp. Serve the round cake in the middle and the petticoat tails as *radii* round it.

F

PARLIES
(SCOTTISH PARLIAMENT CAKES)

1 lb. Flour.	¼ lb. Butter.
½ lb. Brown Sugar.	½ lb. Treacle.
4 teaspoonfuls Ground Ginger.	

Sift the flour and ginger and mix with the sugar. Melt the butter, add the treacle, bring to the boil, and pour on to the dry ingredients. Work up the paste while as hot as your hands can bear it, and roll out to ¼-inch or less in thickness. Mark in squares with a knife or paper-cutter, and bake in a slow oven. Separate the squares while soft and they will soon get crisp.

ABERNETHY BISCUITS

8 oz. Flour.	1 level teaspoon Baking Powder.
3 oz. Butter or Margarine.	Pinch of Salt.
3 oz. Sugar.	1 Egg.
1 scant tablespoon Milk.	

Mix the dry ingredients and rub the fat into them. Beat the egg and add with just enough milk to make a stiff paste. Mix thoroughly and turn the paste on to a floured board. Roll out thinly, cut into rounds and prick all over. Place on a greased baking-tin and bake in a moderate oven for fifteen minutes or until crisp and golden-brown.

GINGER TORTE

6 oz. Flour.	2 Digestive Biscuits.
4 oz. Butter.	1 level teaspoon Ground
2 oz. Sugar.	Ginger.

Cream the butter and sugar. Sift flour and ground ginger together. Crumble the biscuits thoroughly. Work flour and biscuits into butter mixture. Knead thin in two small sandwich tins and bake in a moderate oven for about twenty minutes. Turn out and cool; then sandwich with butter icing made by creaming two ounces of butter with two of icing sugar and a pinch of ground ginger.

PRESERVES

BLAEBERRY JAM

7 lbs. Blaeberries.   **1 lb. Thin Red Rhubarb.**
5 lbs. Sugar.

Pick over the berries and remove any scraps of leaf or stem. Wipe the rhubarb and cut into inch-lengths. Put it into the preserving-pan with the sugar, heat slowly, and boil for ten minutes. Add the blaeberries and simmer, skimming well, until the fruit is tender. Test, and when sufficiently set, pour into dry, warm jars. Cover when cold.

ROSE-HIP JELLY
(FIFE)

Rose-Hips.   **Sugar.**
Crab Apples.   **Butter.**

Use the bright scarlet hips of the wild rose for this jelly. To every breakfastcupful of hips, denuded of their seeds, allow one pound of crab apples. Wash these, and cut into quarters without peeling or coring. Put them in a pan with the hips and water to cover, and simmer till quite soft. Strain through a flannel jelly-bag, but do not squeeze the fruit.

Butter your pan lightly with unsalted butter, pour in the juice, allowing to each pint a pound of the best preserving-sugar. Boil the syrup for ten minutes, or until it jells when tested. Pour into warmed jars, and cover when cold.

This jelly is a lovely rose-colour, and has tonic qualities.

Rose hips should never be cooked in an aluminium pan. Enamel is best.

BRAMBLE AND ROSE-HIP JAM

Rose-hips.
Brambles.

Sugar.
Butter (unsalted).

Allow a large cupful of hips to each three pounds of brambles. The hips, denuded of their seeds, should be finely chopped and left to steep for two days in just enough cold water to cover them. Then wash and pick over your freshly gathered brambles (which should not be over-ripe) and put them into a crock along with the drained hips. Leave in a warmish oven for a day to extract the juice. Butter the jelly-pan, empty the crock into it, and add sugar pound for pint. Finish in the usual way.

This is a delicious bramble jam with a rose-hip flavour.

GREEN GOOSEBERRY JELLY

4 lbs. Green Gooseberries.
A Bunch of Elderflowers.

Sugar.
Water.

Pull the berries while still quite green and hard. Top and tail them, wash, and put into a preserving-pan with just enough water to cover. Bring them nearly, but not quite, to boiling-point, and set aside. Next day strain the juice, measure, and return to the pan with 1 lb. of sugar to each pint of juice. To the same quantity of juice allow three or four heads of elder-flower, and tie them to the handle of the pan so that the blooms float in the boiling syrup. Boil for about an hour, or until the syrup jells when tested. (If the petals are inclined to fall, tie the heads in a muslin bag.) The flowers may be removed earlier if desired. It is best to taste the syrup while boiling to see if the flavour is strong enough. When ready, pour into dry, heated jars.

ROWAN JELLY

Rowan Berries.
Apples.

Sugar.
Water.

Gather the rowan berries when almost ripe. Remove the stalks, and wash and drain the berries. To three pounds of berries allow two pounds of apples, unpeeled and roughly chopped. Turn the fruit into a preserving-pan, and add just enough water to cover. Boil steadily for not less than an hour, and strain through a jelly-bag, being careful not to press the fruit in the least. Measure the juice, and return to the pan, adding a pound of sugar to each pint of juice. Bring to the boil, and boil for half an hour, or until the jelly just sets when tried on a cold plate. Skim well, pour into small pots, and tie down quickly.

Rowan jelly has an agreeable tart flavour, and is an excellent accompaniment to grouse, venison, and saddle of mutton.

ORANGE MARMALADE
(A SIMPLE RECIPE)

2 lbs. Bitter Oranges. **7 pints Water.**
2 Lemons. **8 lbs. Sugar.**

Wipe the fruit, cut in half, and remove the pips. Pass the fruit through the mincer. Put into a basin, cover with the water (cold), and leave for not less than twenty-four hours, Soak the pips in two teacupfuls of cold water. Next day boil the fruit along with the pips (tied in muslin) and the covering water for one hour. Add the sugar, and boil for ¾ hour longer, or until it jells when tested on a cold saucer. Pot, and cover immediately.

SCOTS RHUBARB JAM

6 lbs. Rhubarb. **3 oz. Preserved Ginger.**
6½ lbs. Loaf Sugar. **1 Lemon.**

The red Victorian rhubarb is best for jam, and it should be fairly young. Wipe the sticks and cut into half-inch pieces. Chop the ginger. Wash and thickly slice the lemon, discarding the pips. Place the rhubarb, ginger, lemon and sugar in a large basin, cover closely, and leave in a cool place for three days. Turn the contents of the basin into a preserving-pan and stir frequently until it comes to the boil. Let it boil for thirty-five minutes, then remove the lemon. Pot and seal.

SWEETMEATS

TREACLE TOFFEE

1 lb. Sugar.	1 oz. Butter.
1 lb. Treacle.	1 dessertspoonful Vinegar.

Put the sugar, treacle, and butter into a saucepan, and leave it at the side of the fire till melted. Stir till boiling and simmer until it turns crisp when tested by dropping a little into a cup of cold water. Withdraw, add the vinegar, and pour into a buttered shallow tin. When cool, mark into squares, and when cold, break up.

If preferred, the toffee may be " pulled " immediately it is cool enough to handle. Oil the hands, then throw the toffee over a clean, oiled hook, and pull it rapidly with both hands as long as it is sufficiently pliable. Two pairs of hands do the work even better. When too hard to work longer, cut into pieces with scissors.

ANGUS TOFFEE

1½ lbs. Granulated Sugar.	1 oz. Butter.
2 oz. Ground Almonds.	1 teacupful Milk.

Put the butter into a saucepan, and when it has melted a little, stir in the other ingredients and bring to the boil. Boil for seven minutes, stirring all the time. It soon begins to solidify round the edge, and this must be scraped off repeatedly. Remove from the heat, and continue stirring till thick. Pour into a buttered shallow tin, and when cool cut into bars with a sharp knife. If to be stored, wrap in greaseproof paper.

GLASGOW TOFFEE

4 oz. White Sugar.	1½ oz. Grated Chocolate.
4 oz. Brown Sugar.	½ teaspoonful Vanilla.
2 oz. Fresh Butter.	1 gill Syrup.
2 oz. Salt Butter.	1 gill Cream or Rich Milk.

Melt the butter in a lined saucepan. Add all the other ingredients except the flavouring, and boil, stirring all the time, for fifteen to twenty minutes, or till the toffee turns crisp when tested in cold water. When ready, it will draw away from the sides of the pan. Add the vanilla, and pour into a well-buttered shallow tin. When cool, mark into squares, and when cold, cut through the markings with a sharp knife. Wrap the pieces in wax paper.

This is a toffee of the " Russian " genus that has long been popular in Glasgow.

CREAMY CANDY

2 lbs. Powdered Sugar.   **Pinch Cream of Tartar.**
½ pint Water.   **Flavouring Essence.**

Put the sugar into a lined saucepan with just enough water to dissolve. Cover and boil briskly, without stirring. When it begins to thicken (which will be soon), add as much cream of tartar as may be heaped on a silver threepenny piece. Do not stir, but watch that it does not burn. Try often and speedily by dipping in a small round stick and testing it in cold water. When it breaks short and crisp, pour it out on a buttered shallow pan or ashet, and sprinkle over it the flavouring—vanilla, peppermint, ginger, or other essence. When cool enough to handle, work until white. Cut with scissors into flat sticks, When hard, place in a glass jar and keep a week or ten days, when it will become creamy and delicious.

HELENSBURGH TOFFEE

2 lbs. Loaf or Granulated   **I tin Condensed Milk.**
Sugar.   **I teacupful Water.**
4 oz. Butter.   **I teaspoonful Vanilla.**

Put the sugar, butter, and water into an enamelled saucepan, stir over the fire till melted, then add the contents of the tin (ordinary size), and stir continuously over the fire for forty-five minutes. Remove, add the vanilla essence, and stir off the fire for one minute. Pour into a buttered shallow tin, and when cool, cut into squares.

A halved walnut may be placed in each square.

BEVERAGES

ELDERFLOWER WINE

1 pint Elderflowers.	3 lbs. Loaf Sugar.
1 lb. Raisins.	1 tablespoonful Yeast.
Rind of 1 Lemon.	1 gallon Water.

Put into a pan the water, sugar and thinly peeled lemon rind, and boil for an hour, removing the scum as it rises.

The elderflowers should be freshly gathered and quite dry. Strip them from their stalks, fill a pint measure (packing it loosely), and empty the flowers into a vessel. Pour the hot syrup over them, and stir well. When rather more than luke-warm, add the baker's yeast spread on a piece of thin toast. cover with a cloth, and stir every day until fermentation ceases (about a week). For every gallon of liquor allow a pound of large fleshy raisins ; put them into a cask and strain the wine over them. Next day fix the bung tightly into the cask. Keep in a cool cellar for six months before bottling.

GORSE WINE
(AYRSHIRE)

½ gallon Gorse Flowers.	3 lbs. Demerara Sugar.
1 Orange.	2 oz. Root Ginger.
1 Lemon.	1 oz. Compressed Yeast.
	1 gallon Water.

Simmer the flowers, ginger, and water together for fifteen minutes. Add the sugar and stir till dissolved. Remove from the heat. Slice the orange and lemon, and add to the cooling liquid, and when just warm, float the yeast on a piece of toast on top. Cover with a folded blanket and leave undisturbed for a week; then skim off the head. Strain into a jar, and allow to work for another week; then cork down tightly. A few raisins and a lump of sugar keep it lively. Bottle off in November.

NETTLE BEER

3 handfuls young Nettles.	I oz. Bruised Whole Ginger.
2 handfuls Dandelions.	½ oz. Cream of Tartar.
2 handfuls Cleavers.	I oz. Compressed Yeast.
¼ handful Wood Sage.	Piece of Toast.
	I gallon Water.

Put on the water, and when it boils add the well washed nettles (the common stinging or dead nettle) and the other plants. Boil for fifteen minutes, and strain. Boil up again with the sugar and ginger, and strain again. Cream the yeast, lay it on a piece of toast, and float it on the liquor when luke-warm. When the fermentation is over, add the cream of tartar; then bottle and cork the beer, and place the bottles on a shelf, on their side, in a cool place.

An alternative way to complete the brewing after adding the yeast is to omit the cream of tartar, and let the liquor stand, covered with a cloth, near the fire, till next morning; then remove the scum, and bottle, taking care not to disturb any sediment.

It will be ready for use in a few days.

The old wives consider this a good blood purifier.

PIRR

(SHETLAND)

2 tablespoonfuls Oatmeal.	I teaspoonful Sugar.
¼ teaspoonful Cream of Tartar.	A little Milk.
	½ pint Water.

Mix the oatmeal, sugar, and cream of tartar in a warm jug, and add just enough cold milk to make a smooth paste. Pour in the boiling water, stirring all the time.

This is a refreshing drink, and an excellent cure for a cold if served piping-hot on retiring.

ATHOLL BROSE
(THE LATE DUKE OF ATHOLL'S RECIPE)

4 dessertspoonfuls Heather Honey.
4 sherry-glassfuls Prepared Oatmeal.
Whisky to make up One Quart.

To prepare the oatmeal, put it into a bowl, and mix with cold water to the consistency of a thick paste. Leave for about half an hour, pass through a fine strainer, pressing with the back of a wooden spoon so as to leave the meal as dry as possible. Discard this, and use the creamy liquid for the brose.

Put the dripped honey and the prepared oatmeal into a bowl, and stir with a *silver* spoon till thoroughly blended. Put into a quart bottle, and fill up with whisky. Shake well before serving. If not required at once, bottle, and keep tightly corked.

Another Method : Mix a gill of prepared oatmeal with two tablespoonfuls of liquid heather honey, a gill of whisky and a gill of cream. Serve in wine glasses at room temperature.

BLAAND
(SPARKLING WHEY)

This popular Shetland beverage is simply the whey of buttermilk left to ferment in an oak cask, and used at the proper stage. To make the whey, pour enough hot water on the buttermilk to make it separate, and drain the whey off the curd (which may be pressed and eaten with cream). Pour the whey into the cask, and leave it undisturbed until it reaches the fermenting, sparkling stage.

It is a delicious and most quenching drink, and sparkles in the glass like champagne. After the sparkle goes off it becomes flat and vinegary, but may be kept at the perfection stage by the regular addition of fresh whey.

Blaand used to be in common use in every Shetland cottage, and was at one time given by fashionable doctors to consumptives under the name of the Sour Whey Cure.

INDEX

Other interesting cookery books from Albyn Press

☐ **HEARTY EATING**

From Roy Curtis and Miriam Kahal Hughes, a valuable guide to "coronary cookery" with a fascinating collection of recipes to help keep its readers free from heart attacks. Illustrated by Cecile Curtis/£2·25

☐ **ZEN MACROBIOTIC COOKING**

Now in its fifth big printing, Michel Abehsera's cookbook provides a complete, easy-to-follow guide to one of today's most fashionable styles of eating . . . complete with ingredients, where to get them and ideas for every sort of macrobiotic meal/£1·75

☐ **ASTROLOGY IN THE KITCHEN**

As selected by Cookery Book Club for their members, and a best-seller in America, here are recipes for meals, both attractive to look at and delicious to eat, designed with people's *astrological sign* in mind! By Maria Kozslic Donovan/£2·10

☐ **RECIPES CONTINENTAL**

Ruth Michaelis-Jena's budget-priced guide presents original but simple recipes mainly from north-west and central Europe/48p 'The recipes are short, simple and succulent'—*BBC Woman's Hour.*

AVAILABLE FROM YOUR BOOKSELLER NOW
or from
Albyn Press 3 Abbeymount Edinburgh 8 or
Albyn Press 90 The Broadway London SW19

RECIPES FROM SCOTLAND

FROM THE REVIEWS

" The ideal gift book for Scottish women overseas and for our own at home."—*Edinburgh Evening News*.

" An asset to any kitchen."—*Aberdeen Press and Journal*.

" It lets us, all and sundry, who had not the good fortune to be born north of the Tweed, into many secrets, and solves many difficulties that have slowed our gastronomic march and kept us guessing."—*Food and Cookery Review*.

" I cannot imagine that there can be a single Scottish bosom in which its recipes will not stir nostalgic pangs. The recipes cover every type of dish, but are all genuinely traditional." — *The Scottish Educational Journal*.